HORTICULTURAL TOURISM

HORTICULTURAL TOURISM

By

Charlie Sampson

DISCOVERY PUBLISHING HOUSE PVT. LTD.

NEW DELHI-110 002

Published by:

Tilak Wasan

DISCOVERY PUBLISHING HOUSE PVT. LTD.
4383/4B, Ansari Road, Darya Ganj
New Delhi-110 002 (India)
Phone : +91-11-23279245, 43596064-65
Fax : +91-11-23253475
E-mail : discoverypublishinghouse@gmail.com
sales@discoverypublishinggroup.com
web : www.discoverypublishinggroup.com

***Edition:* 2015**

ISBN: 978-81-8356-946-0

Horticultural Tourism

Printed at:

Infinity Imaging Systems
Delhi

PREFACE

There is strong competition in the travel and tourism business in China. There are many reputable and ethical agencies, and there's the others. It's worth remembering that if an operator is offering a trip which seems amazingly cheap, then the difference will be collected some other way. Sometimes guides and drivers will pay the agency for the right to guide the visitor, ("buying" travelers), and they will then find ways to recover this from the visitors. Sometimes the agency will use non-accredited suppliers, for example for river boats, rather than those which meet the government standard.

The quality of the environment, both natural and man-made, is essential to tourism. However, tourism's relationship with the environment is complex. It involves many activities that can have adverse environmental effects. Many of these impacts are linked with the construction of general infrastructure such as roads and airports, and of tourism facilities, including resorts, hotels, restaurants, shops, golf courses and marinas. The negative impacts of tourism development can gradually destroy the environmental resources on which it depends.

One of the fastest growing tourism ventures in New Zealand today is Farm Stay/Home Stay. Everything from the Hobby Farm to the High Country Station is offering a range of truly NZ "get to know you" opportunities.

Associated with many of these areas are some of the country's best private gardens. In fact, in some cases the garden is the prime attraction.

Blenheim Palace is a large and monumental country house situated in Woodstock, Oxfordshire, England. It is the only non-Episcopal country house in England to hold the title of palace. The palace, one of England's largest houses, was built between 1705 and circa 1724. UNESCO recognised the palace as a World Heritage Site in 1987.

The Royal Norfolk Show is an annual agricultural show, and is held by the Royal Norfolk Agricultural Association. It is the largest 2 day agricultural show in England, and has been held almost every year since 1847. Shows were not held in 1866, 1911, 1934 and 1957. Up until 1953, the show was held at various sites around Norfolk, although it has since been held at a permanent site near Costessey, Norwich, Norfolk. The show tends to be held on the Wednesday and Thursday in week 26 of the year.

—Author

CONTENTS

Chapter–1

INTRODUCTION

Horticulture is the industry and science of plant cultivation including the process of preparing soil for the planting of seeds, tubers, or cuttings. Horticulturists work and conduct research in the disciplines of plant propagation and cultivation, crop production, plant breeding and genetic engineering, plant biochemistry, and plant physiology. The work basically involves fruits, berries, nuts, vegetables, flowers, trees, shrubs, and turf. Horticulturists work to improve crop yield, quality, nutritional value, and resistance to insects, diseases, and environmental stresses. Horticulture usually refers to gardening on a smaller scale, while agriculture refers to the large-scale cultivation of crops. The word horticulture comes from the Latin hortus meaning "garden", and colo (perfect passive participle cultus) meaning "cultivate".

HORTICULTURAL TOURISSM INVESTORS

The Tanzania Investment Centre has invited local investors in horticulture, who are interested in joint ventures with foreigners to submit proposals to the agency for review and promotion of their ventures. An announcement made by the centre towards the week end said the investors concerned must own pieces of land suitable for horticultural project (cut flowers, vegetables and fruit. The announcement said the ideal of horticultural projects should have land size ranging from about 50 ha onwards and which are within the vicinity of water sources for irrigation, and situated in areas with suitable climatic conditions for horticultural investment.

Land information required must include contact address preferably (physical), land size location, availability of water and electricity, legal status of land. air transport accessibility, road, vicinity to important facilities and other important information like climate, soil and rainfall, it said. Meanwhile, the investment agency has also invited local tourism firms or investors who are interested in joint ventures with foreign investors to also submit information on their projects for promotion. According to the centre, the investors must own pieces of land suitable for tourism project like beach hotels, tourist lodges, camp sites, amusement park and sports (golf).

It said the ideal plots of such projects should range from around 20 ha onwards and must be in the areas suitable for tourism. The announcement said the preferred areas should be beach areas, areas near national parks, or any tourist's and attractive areas. It said land information required must include contact address, size and location, availability of water and electricity, legal status, road accessibility, vicinity to important facilities and other important information.

EARNINGS FROM KENYA'S HORTICULTURE SECTOR

The central bank reported on Tuesday that the Kenyan horticulture industry, which also produces fruit and vegetables, earned 70.3 billion shillings (562 million pounds) from exports in 2007. This beat tourism, which earned an estimated 65.4 billion shillings last year, according to the Kenya Tourist Board. Horticulture employs two million Kenyans directly, 80 percent of them small-scale farmers, according to the Fresh Produce Exporters' Association (FPEAK).

"Growth in this (horticultural) sub-sector was buoyed by good export prices of the key export commodities, as export values increased faster than increase in volume of exports," the central bank said in its monthly economic review for February. Horticultural officials said the industry was only slightly affected by post-election violence at the start of this year, which hit the tourism industry badly. A large proportion of the 2007 earnings came from flowers, which accounted for 43.1 billion shillings, or 64 percent. The central bank also said sugarcane output increased by 9.3 percent to 520,100 tonnes in 2007. The bulletin added that the country's current account deficit increased to $1.16 billion in 2007, up from $529 million in 2006, largely due to a $547 million rise in machinery and transport equipment imports.

Ministry of Tourism to Upgrade Malaysia's Parks and Gardens

The Minister of Tourism, Ng Yen Yen, who is a very keen gardener, has decided to use tourism to drive the upgrading of parks and gardens in Malaysia. In August 2010 the Ministry appointed me as Consultant for Parks and Gardens. Since then I have been involved in many site visits and meetings.

My first task was a 'hot potato': to steer the redevelopment of the Water Mall at the Penang Botanic Gardens into a water garden. The grant money had been spend on poorly conceived structures, as a result of which public opinion had turned negative. The Ministry was stung and I had only six months to redevelop the area using the small amount of money left. I hope by June this year to have Victoria lilies and other water plants fully established, and to have a respectable water garden on show.

Next are public gardens in Malacca, Fraser's Hill, Cameron Highlands and Raub to be upgraded. I hear there still others in the pipeline. I hope, during my tenure, to get botanists appointed to take charge of the botanic gardens. We now have public 'botanic gardens' in Penang, Malacca, and Kuala Lumpur that are only botanic in name. With no botanists in charge there are no programmes for research, conservation, interpretation or education. I also want to establish apprentice training schemes for gardeners so as to upgrade gardening as a creative profession.

AFRICA

North Africa

In North Africa we look at the farming practices of the Eggon, a Nigerian hill farming community. The Eggon live in the Mada hills between Lafia and Akwanga. The hills lay between two rivers that Mada and Arikya. The altitude helps retain moisture on the hills due to early morning mists and fogs. The altitude also makes for earlier and longer crop cultivation. They practice bush fallow agriculture as well as mixed farming land management styles. They focus on growing yams, cassava, maize, beans, and African rice; much of what is produced is exported as a cash crop and is their primary source of cash income. The Eggon use a terraced agricultural system to maximize space on the hills. The goats that they raise are kept mostly for fertilizer used in farming. They are only killed on special occasions such as weddings. The Eggon use the diversity in their environment to maximize their production.

West Africa

In West Africa the Kissidougou live on the savannah dotted by dense areas of "forest islands" that was created by the Kissidougou. The Kissidougou practice intercropping within the forested areas. However, they also operate farms maintained on slopes or plateaus that are located between the forest islands. They prepare the savannah lands for forestation through farming and burning of the grasses to fertilize the soils. The Kissidougou graze their cattle on the savannah to help to maintain flammable grasses around the farms and the villages. The Kissidougou create diversity in their environment by farming and transforming savannah into lush, dense forest.

East Africa

The areas of East Africa are one of the most affected by corporate farming. In western Uganda there is a farming society called the Banyankore. Their land is part of the Rwampara hill country, that is between two flat, dry, and less populated areas of land. On the Hills Te average monthly rainfall are 970mm with two short dry months in June and July and a short less severe dry month in January. Seven months out of the year the rainfall is over 1000mm per month. Their primary production are bananas and coffee, they use these as cash crops. Farmers still use substantial areas for millet farming. This is their main food crop. They have intensive home gardens to produce for the families needs and the outlying farming is used mostly for the cash crop production where coffee and banana are cultivated using intercropping methods.

South Africa

In South Africa the conglomerate farming companies has primarily written off the lands in northwest Zambia. The land is mostly made of plateaus with lowers lands in the Kabompo and Zambezi river valleys. Much of the area is in the Congo-Zambezi watershed, the area of land where all water runs into the same river basin. The land has several types of soil. There are areas of yellow clay with higher concentrations of sand where higher rain falls causes soil erosion and makes farming in those areas difficult. There are also areas with fertile red clay that are rich soils good for cultivation of crops. Farmers in the area grow sorghum, millet, sweet potatoes, pumpkin and maize. There is marginal maize production that is used as a cash crop for the community. The area is usually covered by thick forestation that must be cleared before crops can be cultivated, they do not practice agroforestry. Traditionally spouses must maintain their own gardens. The produce is shared communally but the practice leads to intensive home gardens that are maintained by the women of the villages.

SOUTH PACIFIC

Highlander Horticulture

The Enga of the Western Highlands Province in New Guinea receive most of their food from growing sweet potatoes Ipomoea batatas which they plant in mulch mounds at elevations up to 2,700m or higher (Dove and Carpenter 2008). The mounds that the Enga make to plant their crops of potatoes are formed from by piling large amounts of grass taken from fallow, or unplanted, plots then by covering the grass with dirt (Wohlt 2004). The size of the mounds depends on elevation; the higher the elevation; the bigger the mounds will be. Mounds above 2,500m in altitude can have a height of 0:85m in height; while crops below 1,500m are not mounded at all (Dove and Carpenter 2008). The function of the mound is to protect the crops from the frequent frosts that occur at the high altitudes of the Enga. With sweet potatoes having a very long maturation period, 9 months, the Enga also invest their time and space on the mounds with planting other crops that have much shorter maturation periods such as peas in case a heavy frost does claim the crop (Wohlt 2004).

The planting of the mounds is done so that the plants which have a higher frost tolerance, such as the Irish potatoes, are planted casually throughout the mound and the low tolerant sweet potatoes are planted in the best position to avoid the frost. Peas, beans, and cabbage which are all highly tolerant to frost will be planted outside the circle of sweet potatoes and lower on the mound placing them closer to the cold temperatures of the ground (Dove and Carpenter 2008).

The Enga practice fallow rotation where a garden will in crop for about four years followed by about four years of fallow grassland to let the soil replenish (Wohlt 2004).

Garden size for an average Enga garden is about 0.21 hectare or about 2,100 square meters and can contain a few hundred mounds (Wohlt 2004). Another gardening strategy the Enga have implemented is the use of kin lands that are usually within one to two days walk from the farmers normal planting grounds (Dove and Carpenter 2008). The uses of multiple gardens at differing elevation and the ability access clan lands in different areas for gardening have allowed the Enga to adapt to their environment and survive under harsh conditions.

Lowland Swidden Cultivation

Swidden cultivation is an extensive agriculture practice that is also known as Slash-and-Burn agriculture. The process is extensive because it requires a vast amount of land divided into several plots with one plot planted for a period of years, while the other plots lay fallow for a number of years.

For the Bine-speaking peoples of the New Guinea lowlands swidden cultivation is a main practice for crop propagation. The main crop the Bine grow is the taro root, although the grow about 15 subsidiary crops including: sweet potato, banana, manioc, maize, yam, pawpaw, sugar cane, pineapple, and others (Eden 1993). The swiddens which can be placed in either savannas or forests are created by cutting down all the vegetation in the area that the swidden will be. The farmers then pile all of the cut vegetation on the swidden plot and leave it to dry out through the dry season (Hyde 2010). Right before the wet season begins the piles are burned and the soil and ash are tilled together (Eden 1993). The process of tilling the soil and ash mixes the carbon and nitrogen rich ash into the soil thereby fertilizing the soil for the coming crop. After the soil is tilled the crops are planted.

There are two planting years for a single swidden for the Bine farmers. In the first year the Bine plant primary taro root with a few subsidiary crops like bananas and sweet potatoes. In the second year taro root makes up about 50 percent of the swidden and the rest of the swidden is mixed with about 15 other plants. After the second year the Bine farmers move on to a adjacent swidden and allow the previous swidden to lay fallow or unplanted for a period of 5 to 10 years in order to repopulate the vegetation (Eden 1993). The number of years that a swidden will lay fallow is determined by the plants demand for the nitrogen in the soil. Some plants will leach the soil of nitrogen in a few years and require four or five times that fallow; while other plants can be planted for many years and lay fallow only one or two times the planting period (Hyde 2010). Swidden cultivation requires a lot of land in order to feed only a few people, but the Bine, whose numbers are low, make good uses of their land through swidden farming.

Island Horticulture

For most South Pacific Island cultures the main subsistence techniques are hunting and gathering. Fishing and the gathering of sago, banana, and other tropical foods are the norm with very little organized agriculture. The Tabalu of Kiriwina located in the Trobriand Islands practice a form of agriculture called Kaylu'ebila, a form of garden magic (Malinowski 1965). The main crop for the Tabalu is the yam and there is a definite division of labour according to sex when it comes to gardening. Heavy work is done by the men and it includes clearing the vegetation, caring the yam supports, and planting the yam tubers in the ground (Malinowski 1987). The women aid by weeding the gardens.

Gardening for the Tabalu is a very long and in depth magical process; with special magicians and magical ingredients which have been handed down from family member to family member over time. Garden fields which are called Kwabila are fenced in on all sides to keep out the swine that are breed by the Tabalu. Kwabila are then divided into many smaller plots called baleko, these are the individual gardens that the crops will be planted in (Malinowski 1965).

HORTICULTURE IN AMERICA

Prof. Chas. Joly, in the volume of the Journal de la Societe Nation-ale d'Horticulture, pays a liberal compliment to the progress of horticulture in America. He has seen the addresses of 8,000 nursery and seedsmen of America, and regards the successful establishment of a Nurseryman's Association, such as met recently at Dayton, as a mark of horticultural progress well worthy of European admiration. He remarks on the wonderfully active and useful career of our horticultural societies, and shows particularly how much the Massachusetts Society has done for America. Vine culture in the United States is represented truly as having taken a wonderful leap in horticultural progress. He repeats what has been stated before, and seems to give credence to the report that an immense quantity of American wine is sent to France, and there re-shipped to America with French brands, so as to satisfy those who firmly believe only that which comes from abroad can be good for anything. He gives great credit to the governments of those States which encourage science, and especially to those which have appointed State entomologists, whose duty it is to "study all that concerns the parasites of the vegetable kingdom in their several latitudes." Altogether, we have seldom read a more appreciative essay on American gardening than this excellent production of Prof. Joly's pen.

South America

South America consists of modern day Venezuela, Colombia, Ecuador, Suriname, Brazil, Peru, Bolivia, Paraguay, Uruguay, Argentina, and Chile. South America has historically been a land exploited not only for its natural resources, but also for its indigenous knowledge and labor force. The environmental diversification of South America has been at the foundation of its presence in the global economy as a resource for agriculture, forestry, fishing, hunting, livestock, mining and quarrying.

South America can be seen as cultural regions inhabited by Marginal tribe, Tropical Forest tribes, and the Circum-Caribbean tribes each with its own distinct way of agricultural cultivation (Lyon 1974:6).South America's geographic regions are inhabited by regional tribes which include; the Chocó in the Northern Columbian area, The Kayapo in the Eastern Para area, the Chono in the Southern Fuegian area, and the Quechuas in the Western Peruvian area, (Lyon 1974:24). Each of these regions has adapted not only their own cultural identity and agricultural style.

The Southern region of South America is known as the **Fuegian area** and is occupied by the Chono, Alacaluf and Yahgan . These Marginal tribes differed greatly from the other regions in that they were expert in making bark or plank canoes and domesticating dogs, hunting, fishing and gathering. Nomads with simple socio-religious patterns, yet completely lacked the technology of pottery, loom-weaving, metallurgy and even agriculture . Since there was a lack of agriculture in this region the Chono ate native berries, roots, fruits, and wild celery . The source of nutrition for the Chono, Yahgans, and Alcaaluf thus mainly consisted of sea food such as; whales, seal porpoises, guanacos, and otters . The Southern tribes of South America distinguished themselves not in having a rare form of agriculture like the North's slush-mush method or the having intensive agriculture like the East's sophisticated slash-burn method , yet were able to distinguished themselves in being absent of this trait .

North America

A few remarkable farming methods developed by Native Americans were terraces, irrigation, mound building, crop rotation and seeding. Another astonishing plan of theirs was companion planting. These unique techniques produced maximum yielding from their staple crops.

Terracing is an effective technique in a steep sloped, semi-arid climate. The Indigenous farmers stair stepped the hills so that soil erosion was minimal and land surface was better suited for farming. In the Southwest, including parts of New Mexico, Arizona, and parts of Northern Mexico, terracing was extensive. Terraces were constructed by placing rock dams to redirect runoff water to canals that evenly dispersed rain water. The terraced field transformed the terrain into land suitable for farming maize (Keoke and Porterfield 2005, pg. 56). There is evidence that terracing has been used in the Southwest for about 2,500 years (Sandor, Gersper and Hawley 1990, 71). The Anasazi people from this region, built reservoirs and directed rain water through ditches to water the crops in the terraces (Keoke and Porterfield 2005, 58).The natives grew corn, squash, and beans, along with other crops in the terraced fields.

Corn, squash, and beans were staple crops for Native Americans. They were grown throughout much of the North American continent. This trio became known as the Three Sisters. Where they were not grown, the locals traded for them (Berzok 2005, 9). Nomadic tribes, such as the Dakotas, would trade meat for these vegetable staples. The Three Sisters were usually eaten in unison. Fortunately, they provide maximum nutrition when consumed together.

Ancient folklore belief says that the Three Sisters represented three goddesses. Each sister protected one of the three crops. The Three Sisters must never be separated and therefore be planted, cooked, and consumed together—always (Kowtko 2006, 54). This belief turns out to be a good thing. When maize, beans and squash are consumed together, they provide a perfect balance of nutrition. When the trio is eaten together, the body produces a protein that replicates that of meat. This triad was grown together as well. Remarkably, the crops prospered from one another. Geographically, the Woodlands, Prairie, Plains, Great Basin, and Plateau native cultures all utilized the Three Sisters to some extent.

The Indian Triad was an example of symbiotic planting. Native Americans were very good at farming. They found that when grown together, the harvest was much larger than when grown separately. Less land was required as well. The corn stalks functioned as a support for the beans. The beans transferred nitrogen into a usable form for the corn and squash, and the broad squash leaves provided shade for the soil, which aided in preventing evaporation and weed control (Kowtko 2006, 54). As the success of the Three Sisters spread, many cultures turned from their hunting and gathering roots and relied much more on farming (Kowtko 2006, 55).

Another highly successful farming technique of Native American farmers is known as irrigation. This technique was utilized through much of the Southwest and is useful where water is scarce. Irrigation was and is still used today throughout the much of the world. Native Americans became very good at controlling the amount of water that reached their fields. They built long irrigation canals to redirect water from a source to water their crops. The Hohokam people constructed about 600 miles of irrigation canals from AD 50 to 1450 near Phoenix, Arizona (Berzok 2005, 51). Part of the canal is used by the City of Phoenix today. The Olmec of Mesoamerica built canals over 4,000 years ago (Keoke and Porterfield 2005, 55).

Chinampas were invented by Maya farmers. Chinampas are artificial islands in swamplands and lakes. Crops grown on these artificial fields flourished in Mesoamerica.

Mesoamerica was very populated at this time, so they developed this technique for additional farming plots (Keoke and Porterfield 2005, 60). This technique was later used by the Aztec. The Maya and Aztec civilizations grew and flourished due to food surplus.

In the Northeast Woodlands and the Great Lakes region, an advanced society known as the Moundbuilders emerged (Berzok 2005, 13). This society lived in the flood plains of the Mississippi river basin. This culture farmed mainly maize. They had little need for foraging and grew to an advanced civilization due to food surplus. They were the largest civilization north of the Rio Grande.

Storing systems were advanced for the Native Americans. They developed sophisticated storage containers which allowed them to store seeds to plant during the next planting season. They also stored food in dug out pits or holes in hillsides. Native Americans developed corn cribs. These were storage bins that were elevated off the ground. This technique prevented moisture and animal intrusion (Berzok 2005, 122-123).

Seed selection also became advanced. Corn is a domestic plant and cannot grow on its own. The first corn grown by Native Americans had small ears. Only a few kernels were produced. By 2,000 years ago, single stalks with large ears were being produced (Keoke and Porterfield 2005, 55).Native Americans created over 700 varieties of corn by 1500AD.

INDIA

Agri Horticultural Society of India

The society has decided that from now on, the eco lovers to sponsor individual garden sector. Till now RP Modi has sponsored the Japanese Rockery, Bangur Trust has sponsored the model village house, Videocon has sponsored the Rose Garden. RPG has sponsored the garden path illumination.

You can also sponsor individual block of the garden where you may display your banner/advertisement adhering to the specification of the society and without hindering the ecology and aesthetic beauty.

Agriculture Development Trust Malegoan Baramati

The Farm possesses 110 acres of land that is fully under cultivation of crops relevant to the area. The main purpose of the farm is to demonstrate the latest agricultural practices. It also acts as a tool to do applied research on agricultural Technologies & undertake trials before their transfer to farmers. After a careful planning and analysis soil types, the farm was divided in to three major blocks of Horticulture, Agronomy and Nursery unit. This was followed by planting mother plants of horticulture crops such as Mango, Sapota, Guava, Anola, custard apple, pomegranate, figs etc that are mainly grown in the district. The plantation was completed in 1996. Similarly, agronomical crops grown are sugarcane and wheat. Now the entire farm is operated on drip irrigation system for which the water storage tank of 10,00,000 lits capacity has been constructed. The farm has wide collection of mother plants of latest released varieties of horticulture plants.

HORTICULTURAL TOURISM IN CHINA

There is strong competition in the travel and tourism business in China. There are many reputable and ethical agencies, and there's the others. It's worth remembering that if an operator is offering a trip which seems amazingly cheap, then the difference will be collected some other way. Sometimes guides and drivers will pay the agency for the right to guide the visitor, ("buying" travelers), and they will then find ways to recover this from the visitors. Sometimes the agency will use non-accredited suppliers, for example for river boats, rather than those which meet the government standard.

A good agency, such as China Highlights (CHT), does not collect the 'per head' fee, and pay their guides a fixed monthly salary, which recognizes the fact that they are English graduates as well as expert guides. These days the guides expect a good salary as more and more foreign businesses open in China, offering an attractive alternative, and a guide with a good standard of English does not have to 'buy' customers from an Agency.

A good agency does not permit its guides takes their on endless shopping excursions to factory shops. CHT allows it's guides to take it's customers to one "interesting" factory shop per day. This allows the guides to supplement their income through commissions. CHT gets no commissions from these shops but the quality and authenticity of the products is guaranteed.

A good agency believes in delivering value for money, reliable quality, and clarity about what people will get for their money. It will charge a reasonable price, and pay its own staff and suppliers at a reasonable rate.

This, of course, raises the thorny issue of tipping. China has not previously had a "tipping culture" however the practice of tipping guides and drivers has become common practice. Even though CHT pays our guides and drivers a fair salary, they still expect a tip if they provide good service. We provide a guide to the level of tips but in the end it is the decision of the traveler.

China Shenyang International Horticultural Exposition

On 1 st September 2004, Shenyang was officially approved to hold 2006 China Shenyang International Horticultural Exposition (category: A2+B1, professional international Expo) at the 56 th conference of the International Association of Horticultural Producers (AIPH). The Expo will take place from May 1 st to October 31 st , 2006, altogether 184 days. Sponsored by People's

Government of Liaoning Province, Ministry of Construction of P. R. China, Ministry of Commerce of P. R. China, China Council for the Promotion of International Trade (CCPIT), China Flowers Association, and the Expo is to be organized by People's Government of Shenyang and co-organized by Chinese Society of Landscape Architecture and Chinese Association of Park. The Expo will be held in Shenyang Qipanshan Tourism Resort. With the completed South Zone and the North Zone that is under construction in Shenyang Botanic Garden as core areas, the construction for the International Expo will be undertaken and extended to the east and south. The total planned area is more than 5 sq. km, which occupies the largest area compared with previous International Expos.

The construction for the International Expo will be divided into two blocks, Gardening Zone and Entertainment Zone, which is consisted of four parts:

Gardening Show

This is the core of the International Expo, which will be designed and developed further to the satisfaction of AIPH. The construction includes square at the main entrance, 2 outdoor gardens (International Garden and Domestic Garden), 2 indoor exhibition halls (Comprehensive Hall and Tropical Rainforest1 Hall), 20 theme gardens, Feature Flower Street and Green Valley.

Leisure and Entertainment

An entertainment zone will be constructed in the extended area in the east of the Botanic Garden, which will be decorated with flowers, grass and trees, integrating art of gardening with leisure and entertainment, materializing a larruping style of gardening. The landmark architecture is the big performance square, agricultural gardens of different countries, amusement park, children's elysium miniature of world landmarks, world custom street and movie city, etc.

COMPREHENSIVE SERVICE

This part will be integrated into the landscape architecture, which includes tourist reception center, large parking lot, souvenir shop, flower trade center, food street, café and bar, etc.

Exhibition and Activities

Colorful activities of variety will be organized to attract tourists from home and abroad, including celebrations, performance, exhibition and trade, academic exchange ÿ contest and awarding and entertainment, etc.

THEME

We Coexist Harmoniously with Nature

We, together with the nature, constitute the world. Human, blessed with thinking, wisdom and emotion; nature, made up of grass and woods, animals, mountains and waters are all living creatures. We are environment for each other. Harmony makes coexistence possible and coexistence makes future bright.

"Harmoniously Coexistence with the Nature" is our allegation, beckon and stance. It is a great wisdom of promoting Material and Spiritual Civilization with Eco-Civilization and it is the foundation for the sustainable development of human being.

Location of the Expo

2006 China Shenyang International Horticultural Exposition will be held in Shenyang Qipanshan International Scenery & Tourism Development Zone, 20km from the urban area. With Shen-Qi highway (6 lanes), Ma-Song highway, Ji-Xi adjusted highway, Shen-Fu North and Shen-Fu railway meet in this area, the transportation is convenient.

Qipanshan International Scenery & Tourism Development Zone, covers an area of 190 sq. km. Beautiful sceneries changing with times are called by tourists "the original copy of traditional Chinese landscape painting". The Expo will be held in the center of the previous Shenyang Botanic Garden, covering 2.46 sq.km of land as the core area and, 5 sq.km as the background zone.

The Background Zone of the Expo

The background area is to be connected with the Hunhe water system and the core area of the Expo, including an island of 0.6 sq.km. The background area will be built into an ecological zone, and the island will be built for bird protection

Core Area of the Expo

Shenyang Expo will cover 246 ha. of land, which occupies the largest area compared with previous International Expos.

HORTICULTURAL TOURISM IN KENYA

Kenya's exports of 450,000 tons of vegetables, fruit and flowers to Britain and European markets have become the East African country's fastest growing economic sector.

"Kenyan horticulture will bring in $1.3 billion this year. It's come from nowhere in 20 years and receives absolutely no subsidy of any kind and yet it's bigger already than banking, tourism and even telecommunication," said Mark Ashurst, director of the Africa Research Institute, a British think tank which produced a provocative new report on Kenya's horticulture industry. The report, "Kenya's Flying Vegetables," charts the experiences of James Gikunju Muuru, a smallholder farmer in central Kenya. One of 33 siblings, his four acres of farmland — devoted to green beans, tomatoes, cabbage, sweet potato and baby corn — support his wife and six children.

Muuru says he earns seven times as much money from growing green beans and other export crops as he would from growing the nation's staple crop, maize. The money he earns is used to feed his family, as well as for medicine and schooling. His is a common story: Muuru is one of 4.5 million Kenyans who are supported by horticulture, according to the report.

Some detractors claim food security is so pressing it harms Africa to export cash crops, something the Africa Research Institute counters, saying only 10 percent of the total weight of food grown in Kenya is exported and yet it brings in 50 percent of its value. The remaining 90 percent is traded within the region for local consumption.

"Food insecurity isn't about self-sufficiency; it's about having enough money to buy food," said the ARI's Jonathan Bhalla, who researched the report. "Green beans bring in seven to 10 times more money than maize. Africa has been trying for self-sufficiency for years and it's never worked." The report's most controversial point, however, is the argument that buying Kenyan horticulture not only supports the country's developing economy, but it is environmentally more sound than buying locally grown British food. In recent years, the climate change lobby has claimed that the carbon burned up by jetting produce to market uses far too many "food miles." They argue it is much more sound ecologically to buy locally grown produce.

But Ashurst and others argued that it is good for the environment to export Kenyan vegetables by jet. It didn't hurt that they made this controversial assertion to an audience that was dining on sweet potato blinis topped with smoked aubergine caviar, tempura okra and soya bean and chilli cassoulet, all made of produce air-freighted from Kenya.

"Even with air freight, production in Africa is four times greener than produce elsewhere," said Stephen Mbithi, chief executive of the Fresh Produce Exporters Association of Kenya, to guests as they tucked into Kenyan passion fruit brulee with litchi foam, washed down with mango and prosecco cocktails. "Our temperatures are 20 to 25 degrees Celsius all year round; we use no hothouses unlike in Europe, and with two acres there's no space to drive a tractor so we have to use manual means."

African horticultural imports represent 0.1 percent of all of Britain's carbon emissions. Horticultural imports to the U.S. — including Kenyan baby corn, baby carrots, shelled peas and flowers — represent 0.05 percent of carbon emissions. Besides that, more than 60 percent of Kenya's produce is grown by the nation's 1.5 million smallholder farmers, who also produce the high-quality crops thanks to their labor-intensive methods. At least two-thirds of exports are flown out in the hold of passenger flights, meaning they are merely riding on the back of largely tourist travel.

"If you want to reduce greenhouse gasses from planes, you don't look at Africa," said Mbithi. "Total flights from Nairobi are half a percent from Heathrow."

While Africa's carbon footprint works out at one to two tons of carbon per head, in the U.K. it's 11 to 14 tons and in the U.S. it's 22 tons. The U.K.'s government buildings emit more carbon than the whole of Kenya.

Advocates of air-freight argue the climate change lobby is looking in the wrong places.

"Seeing fruit and veg as the epitome of unsustainable consumption eclipses the truth about carbon emissions and sustainable development," said James MacGregor of the International Institute for Environment and Development, a research body. "'Food miles' serves a lot of people very well — the people who use localism as a banner, such as farmers' markets and those in favor of locally produced meat." While websites offer recipes for zero food-miles diets, much of the food-related carbon cost to the environment is hidden by focusing solely on flights, argues the report.

Hothouses to recreate tropical temperatures and clearing Amazon forests to grow soy to feed "produced in U.K." livestock are among the less obvious but more environmentally detrimental factors. Air freight accounts for only 5 percent of emissions from U.K. air transport, asserts the report.

"The idea of food miles is easily understood and it makes people feel they are getting the environmental debate, but the real world is not so easily boiled down," argued MacGregor. "The more the food miles issue gets re-stated, the more the developing country angle gets lost."

A report to the British government last month stresses the need to consider African countries' economies in the lead up to December's U.N. conference on global climate change in Copenhagen. It suggested the British government could pay a "carbon tax" to offset the air freight emissions of horticultural products from developing countries and could provide better consumer information that includes accurate information about the way products have been grown in addition to information about how they have been transported.

GARDENS AND TOURISM CONFERENCE

Marjorie Harris

Marjorie is one of Canada's leading garden writers. She has been the gardening columnist for Canada's national newspaper,' The Globe and Mail' since 1990; makes speeches across the country, was the Editor-at-Large of *Gardening Life* magazine for 12 years and co-hosts tours to gardens in wonderful places, like Italy in the fall of 2009. She has written 15 gardening books, lives and has a plant consulting business in Toronto.

Marjorie's latest book, *Ecological Gardening* will be published in March 2009 by Random House of Canada.

Alexander Reford

Educated at the University of Toronto and Oxford University, Alexander is a historian by profession but turned his attention to gardens fifteen years ago when he left a position at St. Michael's College to run Les Jardins de Métis (Reford Gardens) in Quebec's Lower St. Lawrence region. The great-grandson of the garden's creator, Elsie Reford, he has been instrumental in restoring the gardens and the historic buildings on the property. In 2000, he founded the International Garden Festival, which has been acclaimed by critics and garden writers as one of the premier garden design events in the world. He is the author of several books on the topics of Reford Gardens and Elise Reford. He is presently completing a book on the history of tourism and travel in Quebec and *The Long Walk*, a biography of Elsie Reford. Alexander is the president of the Quebec Gardens' Association and Tourism Gaspésie in addition to being on the Board of Directors for the Canadian Tourism Commission.

CONFERENCE SPEAKERS

Dave Cowen

As a biology undergraduate, David's career began on the front line and then progressed through the operational and business sides of Butchart Gardens. Proud to be associated with a National Historic Site operated by a team of 550 staff receiving one million annual visitors, David is also a board member of Tourism Victoria where he advocates strongly for horticultural tourism.

Roman Dushatsky

In 1988 Roman joined a newly created adventure travel company in the Ukraine. Over the next 12 years he guided tours, developed travel itineraries and supervised operations and product staff. In 2002, Roman joined the Jonview Canada and was appointed Contracting Manager. In this role his responsibilities include researching, negotiating and costing a variety of non-hotel products (activities, sightseeing, transportation, ranches and wilderness lodges, multi-day adventure packages) across Canada. Jonview Canada is the leading receptive tour operator in Canada, handling over 250,000 international visitors annually.

Pascal Garbe

Pascal is one of the best European experts on gardens & tourism. He manages the development of a European garden network shared between France, Luxemburg and Germany, known as "Gardens without Limits". Every two years, on behalf of the Moselle Conseil Général (an authority rather like a Canadian province) he organizes an international Conference on Garden Tourism "Gardens and Tourism - the keys to success". It brings together the world's greatest experts on the subject and has become an unmissable event in Europe.

Pascal has written a great many books on gardens and plants.

Michel Gauthier

Dedicated to showcasing the horticultural wonders of Canada to its residents and the rest of the world, Michel is ex director of the Canadian Tulip Festival and Flora Montreal. Currently he is director of the Rideau Canal Festival, the man behind the VIA Rail Garden Route, director of Canada's first Gardens & Tourism Conference and also hard at work developing an International Garden Festival to be held in Toronto. Michel sits on the Board of Canada Blooms, Ontario Tourism Marketing Partnership Corporation, International Peace Garden Foundation and is Chair of the World Tulip Summit.

Paul Gray

Paul has over 13 years' marketing experience in the cultural sector; working for organizations such as the V&A

Museum and National Gallery in London. He has been involved in the events industry for the last eight of these years - having starting out as a director of a small production company. He now works at the Royal Botanic Gardens, Kew as their Head of Commercial Events, with overall responsibility for over 150 private and corporate events per year, the Summer Swing concert series and winter Ice Rink.

Rogier Gruys

Rogier's team gathers the unique Canadian travel experiences that bring Canada's tourism brand to life, and distributes them to the CTC's marketing, sales and media teams. Previously, Gruys worked in e-marketing, managing the CTC's consumer website.

Larry Hodgson

Larry Hodgson is a freelance garden writer, photographer and garden tour leader. He has lead garden tours to some 30 different countries and has written over 30 books, including *A Gardener's Guide to Canada* and *Les aventures d'un jardinier voyageur: L'Europe*. He won the Perennial Plant Association's 2006 Garden Media Promoter award. Larry currently lives in Quebec City.

Denise Le Gal

Denise Le Gal obtained her Business Management diploma through Malaspina University-College and has been in the tourism industry for 15 years. As Marketing Manager for Tourism Vancouver Island, she is responsible for the development of projects such as our successful Garden Trail publication. Tourism Vancouver Island is one of six regional destination marketing organizations in British Columbia contracted by Tourism BC.

Tom Laviolette

Tom is a graduate from The Niagara Parks Commission School of Horticulture. From 1984 to present, Tom has worked at The Niagara Parks Commission. He has held the positions at the Niagara Parks Botanical Gardens and School of Horticulture which include Instructor, Senior Instructor, Botanical Curator, Superintendent and is currently Acting Director of Niagara Parks Botanical Gardens, Butterfly Conservatory, School of Horticulture and Parks Floriculture. In his present position he is responsible for overseeing the overall direction, maintenance and development of the Botanical Gardens, Butterfly Conservatory and Floral Showhouses, NPC landscapes and NPC plant production. He is also responsible for the overall direction of the Niagara Parks Commission School of Horticulture.

Albane Le Nay.

Albane holds a graduate diploma in organizational information and communications (3rd cycle) from the Université de Bordeaux III and a Master's in tourism from the Université Paris I - Panthéon-Sorbonne and has 13 years' experience in tourism marketing. In her wide-ranging professional career, she has served as marketing and communications officer for different tour operators, account officer for an advertising agency and communications co-ordinator for the Montréal Botanical Garden and Insectarium. She is currently in charge of Market Development - Tourist Clientele for Montréal's Nature Museums, which include the Montréal Biodôme, Insectarium, Botanical Garden and Planetarium. The Montréal Botanical Garden, designated a National Historic Site of Canada in 2008, is considered one of the world's leading gardens. Its 180-acre site is home to a collection of 22,000 species and cultivars, some thirty theme gardens and 10 exhibition greenhouses.

MARY PAT MATHESON

As Executive Director of the Atlanta Botanical Garden, Mary Pat directs all operations for this 30-acre urban garden.

Under her leadership, the garden is actively expanding all aspects of its operations and is implementing a $55 million capital campaign. Mary Pat is also responsible for directing Smithgall Woodland Garden, a 168-acre new and emerging botanical garden in Gainesville, Ga. Among her many awards and accomplishments, Mary Pat was named one of 14 Women of Excellence by *Business to Business* magazine and 25 Power Women to Watch by *Atlanta Woman* magazine, 2005 Professional of the Year by the American Horticultural Society; and the Lexus Leader of the Arts by Public Broadcasting Atlanta.

Prior to joining the Atlanta Botanical Garden, Mary Pat was Executive Director of the Red Butte Garden and Arboretum in Salt Lake City. She is a past president of the American Association of Public Gardens and serves on the board of directors for the Midtown Alliance the Atlanta Convention and Visitors Bureau, the Metro Atlanta Arts and Cultural Coalition, and the American Horticultural Society.

Maureen McIlwain

Maureen McIlwain, grew up in Montréal, with a passion for nature, colour and gardens. A graduate of Ryerson University, she's been promoting Kingsbrae for seven years and has written for *Canadian Gardening* magazine. Maureen and her husband Leslie have two sons and one grandson.

Mark Runciman

Mark joined the Royal Botanical Gardens in 1984, as the Superintendent - Buildings and Equipment. He has held numerous positions within the organization including Director - Physical Plant and Operations, Director - Corporate Projects, Executive Director, and in 2009 was appointed to Chief Executive Officer.

Mark is a graduate of Mohawk College of Applied Arts and Technology (1977) in Architectural Technology and has a National Certificate in Voluntary and Non-Profit Sector

Management. He is a member of the Association of Architectural Technologists of Ontario and the Ontario Association of Certified Engineering Technicians and Technologists. Prior to joing the RBG, Mark was a Project Coordinator for Aiton Power Ltd. a large contracting company that built power station components, water treatment and sewage treatment facilities.

Darrell Schuurman

Darrell joined VIA Rail in 2004, bringing with him over 15 years experience in the tourism industry. Working closely with tour operators, DMOs, and suppliers, he is responsible for increasing market share within the Ontario and Western Canada regions. He works with the various partners to develop new leisure product, and was active in the creation of the Niagara Bike Train and the Spa Train. Darrell completed his Bachelor of Commerce Degree at the University of Calgary. He currently resides in Toronto.

Brenda Sutherland

Brenda is one of six founding members of the 'Rural Gardens of Grey and Bruce Counties'. Membership since 2000 has grown to 29 with the help of Grey Bruce Tourism. They continue to invite gardeners to 'share the rare and diverse garden experiences of their private gardens'.

Linda Thorne

For 15 years Linda Thorne owned and managed 'Thorne & Co.', a store for gardeners in Ottawa. During this time she combined her love of gardens and travel and began leading garden tours to England and Ireland. After closing the store in 2005 she has continued to organize garden tours. In 2008 she offered two tours to Tuscany and France in collaboration with garden-writer Marjorie Harris.

Linda was a member of the Board of Directors of the Canadian Tulip Festival for 10 years and was also a national judge for Communities in Bloom. Prior to opening the store Linda worked as a Policy Analyst for the Federal Government in Ottawa and Vancouver. She has a Master's degree in Public Administration, specializing in Urban Policy.

Eugene Zakreski

Eugene Zakreski is Executive Director of the Stratford Tourism Alliance and leads the product development and marketing for Stratford's tourism and entertainment stakeholders. The goal is establish Stratford as Canada's premiere art town by developing, packaging and promoting its character, culture and cuisine. Eugene has had extensive experience in building travel, hospitality and tourism businesses in North America, Europe and Asia for Air Canada, Mercer Management Consulting, the Ontario Tourism Marketing Partnership Corporation (OTMPC) and The Breeze, the high speed ferry across Lake Ontario. He has led the development and implementation of integrated marketing, advertising and e-communications strategies. He believes the future of tourism is in developing and packaging experiences based on socio-demographic targeting and the primacy of digital media as the means to competitively build tourism businesses.

CHAPTER–2

HORTICULTURAL TOURISM PLANNING GUIDES

Tourism is one of many activities in a community or region that requires planning and coordination. This bulletin provides a simple structure and basic guidelines for comprehensive tourism planning at a community or regional level. Planning is the process of identifying objectives and defining and evaluating methods of achieving them. By comprehensive planning we mean planning which considers all of the tourism resources, organizations, markets, and programs within a region. Comprehensive planning also considers economic, environmental, social, and institutional aspects of tourism development.

DEVELOPMENTAL PLANNING

The serious situation caused by haphazard development has made people and the governments aware of the need for planning of tourism development based on scientific research of the requirements of the travel market and the capacity of the area to take in the tourists. The need for planning is paramount. We do not provide more seats to a plane or rooms in a hotel beyond plane or rooms in a hotel beyond its maximum capacity, taking into account the passenger's comforts. Why should a resort or an area be choked with people?

Planning of tourism development, however, is of recent origin. It was specially taken note of during the last 65 years after public voices were heard against the unplanned invasion of tourism. In 1950, Gerhard Noble called mass tourism "one of the great western plagues hardly less evil in effects than the epidemics of the middle ages." In a conference held in Limuru, Kenya, the tourist inflow was referred to "as a dangerous invasion." These remarks, however, may be exaggerated apprehensions of the environmentalists. But no one disputes the fact that where modern industrial life makes inroads into ancient societies, traditional values begin to totter. Tourism is a form of social industrialisation with all its advantages and disadvantages. Its advantages have to be grasped and utilised with care so that the impact of the disadvantages is minimised. It is here that planning comes in. Planning is of greater benefit to developing societies where tourism is a new phenomenon and has had little or no adverse effect so far. The World Bank warned us as early as 1972:

In many areas of the world, tourism development has produced great disparities in the standards of amenities provided for the visitors and for the local population. This cannot be entirely avoided, but in the long run, the improvement of standards for the local population is probably a condition of successful tourism development. The development of a new resort by the provision of infrastructure costing perhaps millions of dollars has a great impact on land values in the area affected. Were these benefits to accrue largely to a few private landowners, the Bank would have difficulty in financing such a project. The acquisition of land by government or a public agency prior to development... eases the problems of planning on an integrated basis, and of enforcing proper zoning and building regulations. It also helps to ensure that windfall gains do not accrue solely to private landowners and provides the opportunity for the public agency to offer serviced sites to hotel developers at prices which can include, if necessary, an incentive element. There is a very close relationship between land prices and building densities, and by appropriate land pricing the development authority can help to ensure that acceptable physical planning and density standards are maintained.

The statement makes two significant points:

1. Planning should be integrated to avoid as far as possible, disparities in the standards of amenities for the visitors and local population.
2. Tourism planning should not be left totally to private enterprise in search of profit. Government must actively participate in it.

In the past, tourism planning was looked at from a simplistic point of view. Planning simply implied that new hotel construction should be encouraged, more airlines should start operation, promotional campaigns may be launched within the country and abroad and border crossing must be eased. Although it worked to some extent, it was at best an erratic method of planning tourism. That is how most developing countries started their own tourism planning, resulting in a number of mistakes.

Tourism has become a major industry in many countries of the world and has thus a pervasive effect on the economy of the nations as well as their social structure. Unplanned tourism can hamper a nation in getting maximum benefits from its development.

The development of the tourism sector is one of the several options before a government, making claims on its resources which, in most cases, are limited. It is, therefore, necessary for tourism planners to place their case before the government in justifiable terms listing anticipated contribution to the economic development of the country through tourism development. The two economic arguments in favour of developing tourism are:

(a) the contribution in terms of foreign exchange; and
(b) multiple employment potential of the tourism industry. Tourism development has to be planned in relation to the total development of the country and the available resources.

Initially, in the fifties and sixties, most countries except USA were interested in measuring international tourism because this was what mattered to them in economic terms. Meanwhile, USA and subsequently Europe discovered the value of domestic tourism. Its effect on economy was as good as international tourism. In fact, it provided more regional balance than international tourism. In several countries, an annual survey of domestic tourism is conducted and its findings are available to travel industry. Similarly, US Database, a travel research organisation of the USA, has been gathering all kinds of data on domestic and international tourism for more than two decades.

Presently, almost all National Tourist Organisations in developing countries have divisions dealing with domestic tourism. But, only feeble attempts have been made to quantify domestic tourism. For instance, the Government of India has not yet ordered an all-India survey to determine the size and magnitude of domestic tourism. A few Tourism Departments of the State Governments have set up their research sections to quantify the size of domestic tourism in their states.

The following are some reasons for the need of statistical measurement of tourism:

1. Statistical measurement is necessary to evaluate scale and magnitude of tourism to a destination. It can relate to a country, region or a city. The research helps a country forecast future demand over a long period—say, ten years.

2. The results of these researches are important to take decisions relating to physical planning and area development, keeping in view the requirements of the visitors and the local population. In the absence of timely research, a lot more investments will be needed for future expansion. In the sixties, the Government of India built a new airport in Calcutta and by the time it was completed, it was already short of requirements. It was built without adequate research on future demand.
3. Statistical information is required for marketing and destination promotion. The people in charge of marketing want to know which are their prime markets, how market profiles change, information about the emerging new markets, etc.

PLANNING PROCESS

Tourism is part of the services industry. Its importance—economic and social — has to be balanced by a government in relation to the competing priorities of a nation.

A government must take a decision as to whether tourism is important for its economic, social and political interests. And, if the decision is positive, planning based on indepth research is imperative. The economic advantages of tourism are so overpowering that decision in most cases has been favourable. The erstwhile USSR under Joseph Stalin was forbidden to foreign visitors till 1960, but it opened up with a vengeance when Stalin died. The new Russian state immediately switched to international tourism to get its share of the tourist dollar. Other East European states and the newly independent Republics which once-formed part of the Soviet Union are now trying to attract travellers. China was a closed society a decade ago. Now, it is one of the top 15 among the tourist receiving countries, thanks to the massive foreign investments it received from multi-national companies.

While tourism planning is usually thought in terms of developers and promoters in specific projects, it must be seen from national, regional and local levels. Tourism planning and development has to be seen from two levels:

1. The geographical level within which the tourism activity occurs — the destination.
2. At the level of individual operator — resort or a hotel.

Aims and Objectives

Decision at the national level has to be taken by the government, preferably in consultation with various interests involved. A national policy is called for incorporating the directions in which tourism development should take place. The policy should also spell out national goals and objectives. National objectives could be as under:

1. To develop infra and super-structure to provide recreation facilities for visitors and the resident population.
2. Preservation of cultural resources and the heritage.
3. To maximise economic benefits in terms of improvements of standards of living of the people.
4. Generation of new employment.
5. Stimulation of development at regional levels.
6. Ensuring development at tourist centres and resorts consistent with the needs of each area.
7. Maximising visitors' satisfactions.

Affecting Elements

The following are some of the factors which influence tourism development in a destination area:

1. Size of the existing population.
2. Diversity and vitality of already existing tourist activity.

3. Whether the facilities were planned and planted in the area or grew spontaneously because of some man-made or national attraction.
4. Availability of land and finance.
5. Impact on the local community—benefits and social costs.
6. Attitude of the local people towards the tourism projects.
7. Magnitude and speed of development.
8. State of the local economy — options of alternate development.
9. Availability of local manpower — a dynamic population.
10. Whether the area is extensive for future expansion or only limited expansion is possible.

Resentment by local population against tourism projects, however beneficial to the community, can create problems, as it happened in Australia. Yeppon is a small town on the coast of central Queensland—Australia's sunshine state described by its 6,000 inhabitants as 'Paradise'. It has beautiful views and miles of glorious beaches. A Japanese businessman saw the area and fell in love with it, deciding to develop it into a resort. The beach here is 10 times longer and wider than Waikiki in Honolulu. He bought 20,000 acres to develop it into an international resort, building a number of hotels, guest houses, wildlife parks and several other attractive features.

The scheme was approved by the Australian Government but the local residents did not like it. They could not tolerate the idea of thousands of tourists crowding their beaches all the year round.

The investor tried to woo the local population, offering them millions of dollars to build a retirement home and other facilities. In November 1981, a bomb exploded under a motel under construction destroying property.

This is an example of the type of problems a developer can face — if local cooperation is not sought.

The Prerequisites

As discussed earlier, research is a precondition for planning in tourism. It is surprising that in the tourism field, an insignificant amount of money is spent on research compared to total turnover of tourism earnings.

The spectacular tourism development in certain areas like Majorda in Spain or Hawaii in the United States was due to the fact that these were some of the first areas developed for a particular type of holiday. Today, they are no longer alone in the field. The sun, sea, sand and reasonable prices are available at other places too. Fast jets have made inexpensive travel possible to distant lands — like Sri Lanka, India, the Maldives, Thailand and Malaysia — where prices are much lower. Therefore, for any new resort development, planning, both physical as well as economic considerations, are essential.

A country which decides to develop tourism should take a hard look at places offering similar attraction, study their economics and call for specialists to prepare a tourism development plan. Competition must be identified.

Technical assistance from foreign experts is useful as they can provide an objective assessment of the tourist resources of a country. Among the aspects to be studied are:

1. Characteristics of the land available for development, and the price structure.
2. Speed of construction to attract public investment.
3. Composition of the facilities to be provided — hotels, non-hotels and other services, industries like restaurants, stores and beach services.
4. Total cost of infrastructure and superstructure in the area proposed to be developed. Infrastructure includes all forms of construction on and below the

ground, that is, roads and parking areas, railway lines, airports, water supply, power houses and sewage disposal. Superstructure consists of hotels, motels, restaurants, entertainment, and shopping facilities.

5. Possibility of direct and indirect taxes from tourism-related activities to justify public investment.

Stages of Planning

Planning has to be done on two levels — national and local. At the national level, the central government will be involved in developing selected areas on the basis of research and study. The guiding principles in the selection of the areas are their marketability as tourist spots to international and domestic travellers, anticipated receipts from the tourism sector, and projections of future demand. The national plan shall also lay down the broad framework for development at local and regional levels.

The detailed planning of the local needs has to be done at the local level though the central government may give financial assistance or subsidies to some of the activities. This arrangement is prevalent in countries where tourism is not highly developed and the state has to play a pivotal role. In India, although the government is involved in tourism planning, the private sector plays a significant role in developing tourist facilities. Some of the facilities are planned, developed and managed solely by the state. Now, most countries including China have opened their tourism sector for private participation.

It may, however, be understood that a government cannot afford to do everything at once. They have to select priority areas for development where some infrastructure may exist and whose tourist attractions are relatively better known. The development of completely new areas, though a worthwhile proposition in time, has to take its turn depending upon the resources of the country and the political will to develop tourism on the part of the government.

In October 1977, the World Tourism Organisation published an inventory of tourism development plans of various countries. Out of the forty-three member-countries, which replied to the WTO questionnaire, thirty-seven had an integrated planning system at the national level. But in majority of the cases, the plans remained on paper and when these were acted upon, action was half-hearted or partial implementation. Some countries, like the United States and Canada, have, strictly speaking, no national tourism plans. In the USA, a study for making federal policy and programme involvement in tourism more coherent and responsive to national interest was undertaken only in 1976. After six years of intensive efforts by the travel industry, President Ronald Reagan signed into law a National Tourism Policy Act on October 16,1981. Under this Act, the US Congress created the US Travel and Tourism Administration to 'optimise' the contribution of tourism and recreation industries to economic prosperity, full employment and international balance of payments to the US. In 1996 USTTA has been axed in an economy drive by Clinton Administration. In Canada, each of the ten provinces and two territories are involved in tourism development planning. In USA, states are more actively involved in the promotion of tourism even more than the federal government. France has a full-fledged Ministry of Free Time which deals with tourism and leisure affairs.

Combined Planning

There has been little coordination and regulation in physical planning for tourism development. Resorts have developed in attractive settings while ancillary facilities like transportation were created belatedly to meet the demand. Industrial and commercial cities found themselves receiving more visitors. The new, substantial facilities created were shared by foreign visitors and the local people. Existing infrastructure designed for the requirements of a relatively static age came under the strain of a new and mobile society. The need for replanning of the existing use of land and planning of new areas became paramount. This realisation, however, came only in the second half of the twentieth century. Simultaneously, the transport revolution opened new parts of the world for touristic exploration.

The tourism planners, therefore, had two different tasks — one of physical planning in new areas with potential but with little or no existing touristic activity, and the other of re-shaping the areas where tourism already existed. Two, replanning of existing high density tourist areas.

Where should the planners begin? The first thing is to analyse different types of national or other tourist resources — of which each country has many — that could attract tourists. These may be of scenic beauty, history, a mystique, and so on. An inventory of all these resources of the country has to be made. Then, there are cities like London and Paris which have their own natural draw for visitors. London, the biggest tourist attraction in the world, is visited by over 10 million tourists and Paris by about 20 million foreign visitors annually.

After preparing the inventory, areas have to be selected for tourism development keeping in view the economic resources available. While taking up the areas for development in a city, it is necessary to define the minimum urban planning parameters which, if respected, may prevent the degradation of the environment through unregulated building activity. The Mediterranean seacoast is an example of such unregulated development leading to ugliness and confusion.

The basic parameters in planning a sea resort should indicate (a) the space between buildings, (b) the distance of the road from the beach; and (c) the capacity of tourist accommodation on the beach or off the beach.

The guidelines should also give building specifications, length, suggested dimensions, and characteristics of the road network providing access to the sea. The creation and development of a green belt should be clearly marked. No unregulated or unplanned structures should be allowed in the area proposed to be developed. Similarly, the tourism development plan of an area with historical monuments as a major attraction requires that the view of the monuments should not be concealed by any haphazard construction in the area surrounding the, monument. For instance, no new construction should be allowed near the Taj Mahal, which may obstruct its view.

To sum up, the following must be considered in any area planning:

1. Preparation of overall inventory of national tourist resources.
2. Determination of broad parameters of urban planning and architectural specifications.
3. Cost benefit studies of the proposed projects.
4. Exploration of possibilities of investment in private and public sectors.

Investment and Income in Tourism Development: When a tourism project is taken up for implementation, the time relation between investment requirements and revenue expectation has to be kept in mind. The chart on this relationship and the involvement of the public sector in this chapter explains the position.

The following 8-point project structure for tourism planning and development is recommended:

1. Establishment of goals after a feasibility study.
2. Market and resources analysis.
3. Conceptual planning.
4. Approval of the plan.
5. Master planning.
6. Staged implementation programme.

7. Evaluation and direction.
8. Monitoring operations to ensure quality of services and operational success.

Systems must be set up to provide continuing feedback on volume of tourism and levels of satisfaction provided. Such programmes are directed against decline of a destination.

Role of Government

To make a tourism plan work, Governments have to create a favourable climate for investment through regulations and fiscal measures. Since most private investors would expect a reasonable return on investment, special financial incentives are necessary to make tourism investment attractive. A tourism project needs to be assisted at two stages: first at the time of making investment, and subsequently at the operational stage. Participation in the development of a tourism plan by government may be more attractive to investors, if the government offers direct financial subsidy.

Another form of help is special credit facilities for tourism projects as in countries like UK, France, Spain and India. A common form of credit is long-term loans for hotels at less than the market rates of interest. Since tourism financing is different from other industries, some countries have created special institutions to disburse such loans. France has Caisse Centrale de Credit Hotelier; Portugual has its Tourist Fund, Israel its Tourist Industry Development Corporation. In India, hotels are financed, on the recommendation of the Department of Tourism, by Industrial Finance Corporation of India (IFCI) at central level and State Financial Corporation at state level.

In the late eighties, an India Tourism Finance Corporation (TFCI) was created to finance tourism projects and it is doing a good job. Other organisations also continue to finance tourism projects. Tourism related industries could have a preferential rate of interest. Other alternate measures could be grant of interest rebate on tourism investment by making up the difference between the commercial rate and the rate proposed for the hotel industry. This is one of the several incentives given to hotels in recent years in India. Special facilities for the purchase of land at concessional rates for tourism superstructure can be a powerful incentive — specially in the backward regions of the country.

Some governments recognise tourism as an export industry, as in India lately and offer same fiscal benefits and incentives as are available to other export industries. These include duty free import of equipment required for tourist services or reduction in customs duty or their waiver. The government can also make tourism investment attractive by giving tax relief at the operational stage to improve profitability. No tax for the first 2 to 5 years.

The following chart explains the relationship between tourism investment and revenue derived from it once it is developed. The Government can help tourism planning through manpower development by running hotel and tourism training schools/courses. Finally, the extent of government concessions to tourism is basically linked with the importance a state attaches to the tourism sector compared to other sectors of economy. The involvement of the government in tourism planning, development and promotion varies from country to country.

Government Tourism and the Ambiance : The control of planning of physical environment in tourism is imperative. The following points must be taken into consideration:

(a) What facilities should be erected and when?
(b) Alternative uses of land
(c) Pollution
(d) Serenity of atmosphere
(e) Integrity of landscape

(f) Cost of land and its ratio to building and development costs.
(g) Traffic circulation
(h) Zoning and density
(i) Services — water, electricity, gas, sewerage, etc.

Architectural style, building regulations, site-layout density, and preservation of the natural features of the land are part of the environmental control. Protecting lakes, hills, beaches, rivers and historical monument from the onslaught of large masses of visitors are also the responsibility of the government.

A couplet in the Atharvaveda says: "Whatever I take from the Earth may that have quick growth again. O Purifier! may we not injure the vitals of Thy heart."

The Atharvaveda pronounced these words of wisdom more than five thousand years ago when Indian culture was being formed in the magnificent forests teeming with wildlife. It is remarkable that people in that age realised that the resources of the earth were not something which could be damaged at will. The following words of philosopher Krishna Chaitanya provide another warning:

If we do not realise that the beauty and variety of the earth are autonomous values in their own right, if we believe that we have life and health on earth and not with the earth, we will exploit it greedily and come to ruin speedily. If we treat the earth without reverence and ruin its beauty and order, the end will be the failure of the earth to produce any food for us.

Demands for tourism are as diverse as the resources. It is not easy to match the supply with the demand, for tourism can create pressure on local facilities; can affect the landscape and the life-style of the people.

The problems of conservation were taken note of in the early stages of tourism development. America established the Yellow Stone Park within an area of 3,350 square miles in 1872. The British founded a national trust for places of historic interest and national beauty in 1895. A separate Ministry of Town and Country Planning was created in 1943 in Great Britain. National Physical Planning began in the United Kingdom as early as in 1947 with the passing of Town and Planning Act. The National Park Access to the Countryside Act in 1949 established a National Park Commission with the objective of natural beauty and provision of opportunities for open-air recreation. The ten national parks created in England covered nine per cent of the land area. In 1971, a Department of Environment was set up in England. In India, too, a Ministry of Environment and Forests was set up when Rajiv Gandhi took over as Prime Minister in 1985.

The concern for preservation of ecological balance was not confined to the USA and the UK; it has its worldwide impact. In 1968, the Council of Europe launched the Air Pollution and Water Charter and Water Conservation Campaign. The African convention for conservation of nature took place in the same year. In the USA, the Council of Environmental Quality was established in 1970 and President Nixon promulgated a 37-point programme of preservation of environmental quality.

India is already facing problems relating to environment mainly due to pressure of population and only partly due to tourism. The case of Dal Lake in Srinagar (Kashmir) proves our point.

Tourism can be a boon to any country, especially to a developing country like India. But tourism planning has to ensure that India preserves the Himalayas in their original glory, and the wide variety of wildlife, which is a great asset for tourism. The government took a wise decision in banning the hunting of tiger, panther and other species which were in danger of becoming extinct due to wanton killing. The Tourist Development Council, an advisory body of the Government of India, in a resolution passed as early as 1972 at Goa, requested the Government of India to take steps to ensure that:

(a) Any new construction in the vicinity of monuments should meet aesthetic requirements.

(b) Any unnecessary interference from electric lines, power plants, petrol stations, advertisement hoardings be avoided.

(c) Special care should be taken to prevent pollution of water and air, working of mines and quarries, dumping of domestic, commercial and industrial waste in the vicinity of monuments.

(d) Deforestation of the area around monuments be avoided.

(e) Financial assistance be given by the state governments, local bodies to improve and beautify roads and environment of monuments and other places of tourist interest.

(f) To avoid haphazard peripheral growth, the location of facilities like canteens, bookshops, curio shops, etc., in the vicinity of important monuments may be done only after clearance from the Archaeological Survey of India and the Department of Tourism.

As a follow-up on this resolution, the Department of Tourism selected ten archaeological complexes of tourist importance comprising thirty archaeological centres. Master plans for these have already been prepared.

Concerns of Tourism

As part of the concern for tourism in relation to environment, WTO conducted a survey of tour operators in United Kingdom about their views on environments.

To a question whether tourists were concerned about the environmental quality of the destination they visit, 63 per cent of the tour-operators surveyed answered yes.

In reply to another question whether they offered any products that might be classed "environmental friendly" or

"Green", 61 said yes. Seventy-nine per cent of the group said that they offered green products in Europe, 16 per cent in Asia Pacific, 13 per cent in Americas and 37 per cent in Africa.

It seems that tour-operators were taking their business to alternate destinations from areas where environmental degradation was accentuating. Fifty-nine per cent said that they were moving their business from areas where environment was not safe.

Marketing Planning Marketing Concepts

What we have been discussing until now is information of the environment in which the advertising campaign will have to work. As we know, since advertising is only the communication aspect of the total marketing function we have to take into account the marketing plans of the both enterprises in the long-term and short-term, and relate the advertising to these. The marketing objectives that are given by the enterprise will detail the plans that the enterprise has for its product in the coming year and in some cases for a few years ahead. These plans would cover items such as:

(i) The sales targets for the coming years broken down into regional targets or others, as the case may be.

(ii) The distribution, merchandising and sales promotion activities planned to support the sales increase;

(iii) The role that advertising is expected to play in creating consumers;

(iv) The inhibiting factors which will work to prevent the enterprises from achieving the target, competitive products and their advertising, consumer attitudes, etc.

It is important to note that in any marketing operation the product formulation, packaging and pricing, distribution and availability at point of sale are all of vital importance. All that advertising can do is to bring consumer to the point of sale. But if the product is not properly made, packaged or priced or is not well merchandised or promoted at point of sale and, therefore, is not visible, then it is quite possible that the sales effect of the advertising will not fructify. This brings out the importance of integrating these various activities.

Once we have got clearly the marketing objectives of the enterprise and their plans in relation to these objectives, we can see what advertising has to communicate and to whom with a view to provide the maximum relevant support to the agreed marketing plan.

Campaign Planning

We now know what we have to sell, to whom we have to sell, where the prospective consumers are located and also how the product will be made available to them. Our object now is to create an advertising campaign which will reach target audience and motivate them to come to ask for and buy the product. We have now processed all the facts that the enterprise has given and have perhaps had a dialogue with the consumer, through research, to ascertain his knowledge, attitude and usage of the product and its competitors. As a result, we have found out the proposition that we feel would be most motivating. We have also found out where the consumer is located, how and when he buys the product. We are now in a position to get down to work on two aspects which make up an advertising plan. These aspects are: (i) the creative strategy and (ii) the media plan

Creative Strategy: Creativity in advertising is very crucial as on this depends the comprehension of the customer to understand the product. We now have to transform proposition or statement into an idea which is to be communicated to the customer. In converting the proposition into an idea, use of creativity is of paramount importance. Creativity must take into consideration direction and relevance. For the bright idea to be useful, there must be a right idea. It is this idea which has to be communicated to target group. In order to communicate the idea, media personnel, production personnel as well as creative personnel will have to be involved in this area. Finally the idea will have to be channelised into various material that will be required for advertising campaign. This can range from press advertisements to film commercials, to radio spots and TV spots, to posters and other point-of-sale material. All these items will be creative interpretation of the idea.

The Media Plan: While creativity is perhaps most closely related in an agency with the development of an idea and its interpretation into advertising material, it also plays a role in the development of a media plan. Let us know briefly the way in which an agency constructs a media plan. Media may be defined as vehicles of mass communication which are used to carry advertising messages. Very rarely, except in the case of direct-mail advertising, are media developed solely as advertising communication vehicles.

One may broadly classify media into two groups:

(a) Media which are read, seen or heard by the consumer for their 'editorial' worth. These are the newspapers, magazines, the radio programmes cinema shows, TV programmes which are read or tuned into or watched by the consumer for the 'editorial' material which they offer. The advertising benefits from the editorial climate of this media.

(b) Media, usually more 'reminder' type of media such as outdoor media, hoarding, transportation signs, posters, kiosks, neon signs, etc., which are noticed in passing only. They obtain consumer exposure due to the fact that the consumer's living habits cause him to pass by them. For instance, commuters in trains and buses, motorists and pedestrians on roads are all exposed to such media.

The above group also includes point-of-sale items. In preparing media plans one has to study the behaviour and exposure of consumer groups with regard to both kinds of media. We have to study both kinds of media. We have to study what media our target consumer looks at for 'editorial' pleasure and when he does so and in what frame of mind. By studying consumers living habits and pattern of movement we can assess which of the second group of media he will be exposed to as a general rule. In the more advanced countries it is possible to get detailed statistics on the kind of audience that each medium has. In advanced countries this information is very detailed indeed and permits one to prepare accurate media plans. In other countries, however, this information is still very scanty and apart from basic circulation information it is rare that one gets much else. However, through experience one gradually builds up a fund of knowledge which enables one to select appropriate media for appropriate markets. Here, apart from the circulation information a study of the quality of the medium in terms of editorial content and style is a very useful method of evaluating reader types.

CHAPTER–3

HORTICULTURAL TOURISM MANAGEMENT

We have the domain proficiency in offering Horticulture Management Services to our clients. Owing to our recruitment provisions for gardener, we are successful in providing well-trained gardeners to our customers. The gardeners are recruited by us on their experience and knowledge in their respective domain.

MANAGEMENT ART

It is the art or science of getting things from people. The concept was born in the USA after the completion of Hawthorn Studies during the thirties of the last century. It has become the most widely read and practised field of learning in the world today. The objective is of prime importance while a person manages his affairs, people, things or abstract concepts. The manager is an important person in an organisation and not the one who is being managed. But for the manager himself, the persons being managed and directed assume more importance because he has to get outputs from them. Management pervades all the areas of human endeavour.

Concept of Business Management : It is a field of human thought in which, individuals and groups try to earn profits out of industrial, commercial and service ventures with minimum possible inputs. The resources at the disposal of a business enterprise are scarce. The business manager must use them in an optimal manner to produce the best results (maximum profits) for himself or his group (the firm).

The current trends of the global markets are pointing to the fact that most of the business management operations would create and support the most revered and sought after activity-entrepreneurship. Thus, individuals or small groups would seek to capture the local, regional and global market niches. They would have to communicate with such niches with the alacrity of the speed of light. That is how, they would be able to survive in the jungle of business.

Concept of Marketing Management : According to Phillip Kotler, marketing management takes place when at least one party to a potential exchange gives a thought to the objectives and means of achieving the desired responses from the other party.

Thus, we are clear about the concept of two parties in the process of exchange. Both these parties engage in transactions after the process of exchange is over. One of them has some objectives to achieve within the framework of an organisation, Thus, marketing management is essentially a managerial activity if one of the participants in the process of exchange works for meeting such objectives as are more vital and pious than the immediate results that would be achieved through the completion of transaction at hand.

Thus, marketing management may be defined as "the process of planning and executing the conception, process, promotion and physical distribution of ideas, goods and services to effect exchanges that satisfy individual and organisational objectives. "

According to American Management Association's *AMA Handbook,* the following guidelines are vital in the context of the success of marketing management in the firm:-

(A) Know your markets.
(B) Plan for changes in your market niches.
(C) See new opportunities and convert them into profits.
(D) Develop different (suitable) product mixes for different markets.
(E) Carry out more new product testing exercises.
(F) Increase your market shares in crisis markets.
(G) Expand your product mix and add value to it.
(H) Use Value Addition (VA) techniques to get the desired marketing results at minimum costs.

Global markets are created by making the prospective clients aware of the products and services of the firm. These markets are catered to by motivating the prospective clients (of these markets) to purchase the goods and services demanded by them. These markets are retained by informing the clients (of these markets) that the products and services they had bought are the best in their respective categories. Finally, these markets are expanded either by giving information to the clients (of these markets) about changes and modifications in the existing products, or by introducing new products in these (same) markets.

So, the objective of a marketing team would be to :

(a) inform the prospective customers about the products or services of the firm;
(b) persuading them to buy those products and services that satisfy their demand.;
(c) convincing them that they have purchased the best products or services; and
(d) reminding them to purchase the same, modified or new products of the firm.

Thus, these four communication exercises form the essential building blocks of the edifice of marketing. We shall study later that these are the four rudiments of the most powerful communication exercise on the earth that is known as Advertising.

Horticulture Tips to Minimize the Impact of Water Stress

1. Popularization of micro irrigation system: Micro irrigation more popularly known as drip irrigation is an important strategy in reducing the impact of drought. The main feature of micro irrigation is the high level of efficiency in water use coupled with higher yield. If you use the same quantity of water used in conventional methods of irrigation, nearly two times more land can be irrigated through the drip system.

2. Use of mulches: Soil moisture can be conserved through mulching with black polyethylene or locally available mulches, growing cover crops or inter-culturing in the orchards. These methods also check soil erosion and runoff of rainwater. Application of farm yard manure or vermin-compost for improving soil health and water holding capacity of the soil is another way to efficiently use and conserve the water that is available. Sometimes plants are covered with mulches preferably grass mulch (10-12 kg/ basin) and black polyethylene mulch (100 micron) throughout the growth period. This helps in conserving soil moisture, saving water for more critical stages and reducing the weed population by 60 per cent with grass mulch and 100 per cent with polyethylene mulch. This reduces the cost of cultivation.

3. Use drought tolerant rootstocks for Horticultural Crops: One tool that has played an important role in making India one of the leading producers of fine quality grapes is the use of rootstocks. Rootstocks offer attractive and environmentally sound protection to vine and grapes in conditions of severe shortage of irrigation water and uncertainty of rainfall. Many rootstocks have been introduced and tested at Indian Agricultural Research Institute (External website that opens in a new window),

New Delhi and Indian Institute of Horticultural Research (External website that opens in a new window) in Bangalore. Two rootstocks that display the most potential are Dogridge and Salt Creek. Rangpur Lime is one rootstock that is tolerant to drought. It is also capable of bearing Phytophthora and salinity. This rootstock is recommended for areas in which the Rough Lemon rootstock is currently in use because of the large amount of water it saves.

4. Use of shed-nets in nursery: Keeping nursery plants under shed-nets and irrigating them through micro-jets facilitates their survival percentage and reduces irrigation needs.

5. Rain water harvesting: This method consists of in situ water harvesting through the opening of small trenches and contour bunding. Another technique of rainwater harvesting is the use of micro irrigation systems whereby rainwater is collected in the lower regions of the farm and later recycled to the crops.

HORTICULTURE BUSINESS

The modern horticulture business can be one of many enterprises that service a broad clientele. From the greenhouse business that caters to retail customers to the commercial wholesaler who provides landscaping products to builders and retail garden centers, the desire for flowers and shrubbery continues to be in great demand. Starting a horticulture business requires specific horticultural know-how as well as basic managerial and business knowledge. Both can be learned through first-hand experience as an employee at another business or through college courses, county extension service programs or self-teaching.

Instructions—Write a comprehensive business plan. Like all start-ups, the horticulture business suffers from an 80 percent failure rate within the first five years of operation. A traditional business plan will focus on the requirements of your business, your immediate competition and your risk and reward.

Get financing. With your comprehensive business plan in place, make applications to lenders for financing that you will need until your sales are able to sustain your business.

Decide on the location for your business. Either purchase it or lease it. A retail business must have an easily accessible location while a wholesale enterprise will require trucking access. Both types of businesses need adequate space for growing plants as well as access to electricity, water and heat.

Get the appropriate permits and licenses. Most jurisdictions require occupancy permits and business licenses. You must also get your Federal Tax Employer Identification Number (EIN) as well as your state and local sales tax licenses.

Open a business bank account and set up at least two different major merchant credit card accounts.

Apply for business credit with suppliers, shippers and business-related vendors. The success of your business will depend on your ability to quickly purchase raw material, ship the product if you are a wholesaler and take advantage of discounts and preferential client statuses.

Stock your shelves with products purchased from your wholesalers and display plants grown in your greenhouse and field.

Advertise your business. Customers can't spend money with you if they don't know you exist. According to the Small Business Administration, many businesses fail because of their owner's neglect to market their services and products vigorously and continuously.

Tips & Warnings—According to the University of Arkansas' Division of Agriculture, a population of 6,500 people will marginally support a one-greenhouse retail horticulture business. Using this formula and noting the number of active competitors servicing that population, you will be able to calculate the size of your new business.

How to Plan a Horticultural Retail Business

If you love plants and have a passion for retail, then a horticultural retail business could be perfect for you. But before your start your business, you will need to lay out a solid plan. Starting a horticultural retail business entails making a lot of decisions, such as what kind of retail outlet you will operate, who you are marketing your products to and how you will finance your business. Writing a business plan will help you, and others, to understand how you plan to start and run your business.

Instructions—Write an overview of your business plan. This is often referred to as an executive summary. Its purpose is to give people a quick understanding of your business without going into great detail. It can also be useful as a way of reminding you what your overall objectives are. The plan describes how you will operate, what kind of retail location you will use, what type of plants you will sell and what your expected costs and profits will look like. All of your overview descriptions should be written on a broad level, reserving details for the body of your plan.

Draft the body of your business plan. Here you will describe business operation details such as who the managers will be and their relevant horticultural and retail experience. You should also explain the market to which you are selling plants, what kind of plants your customers buy and how they purchase them. You should then explain your plan for marketing your business to these customers through media, advertising, promotions and other means. Finally, you should provide financial details such as the cost of purchasing plants, the price you expect to sell them for and overhead costs such as rent, utilities and wages. You should estimate your cash flow and your profits for your first year of operations and explain how your business will be financed.

Attach relevant documents as an appendix to your business plan. Relevant documents might include plant price lists from suppliers, financial details about similar horticultural businesses and market research about consumer trends in horticulture. The purpose of this section is to provide documentation that supports what you have said in the body of your business plan in order to allow people to find detailed information that they might require.

Tips & Warnings—Remember that planning a business is an ongoing endeavor. You should treat a business plan as a living document and make changes to it over time.

How to Start a Greenhouse Business

Starting a greenhouse is like starting a factory—one in which the product is terminal at every stage of the process. The greenhouse owner makes a 24/7 commitment to care and management of product and personnel. You need experience in business management as well as horticulture to run a successful greenhouse business.

Instructions—Decide which crops you plan grow. Base your stock on what sells, not just what you like. Check your local sellers and verify what they are selling, and what they aren't selling. Analyze your competition and look for their weaknesses. Choose between bedding plants, flowering potted plants, potted foliage plants and cut flowers. Odds are you may choose to deal in several types of stock, not just one. Be sure you have the room to move between different types of stock.

Choose your site. Things to consider when selecting a site are zoning restrictions, proximity to utilities, unlimited water supply, strong customer and worker base, roadways and topography. Choose the site that requires the least amount of altering, has not more than a 5% slope and has a natural windbreak but is still clear of summer and winter shadows.

Select your greenhouse design. This includes the structure and type of covering, as well as climate control systems, flooring, benches and germination areas/heat systems. Design your site plan. You need to create a site that is conducive to maximum production. Things to consider are deliveries, loading and unloading areas, work and storage space, customer access and sales. Keep in mind that you may need to expand in all of these areas as your greenhouse business grows.

How to Start a Tree Trimming Service

Starting a tree trimming service can be a great way to earn some money, spend time outdoors, and do your community a service by cleaning up overgrown trees. There are opportunities to get business contracts, residential contracts and government contracts with your specialty tree trimming services. Running a successful tree trimming business requires business knowledge and horticultural education. Having a degree or certificate in botany or horticulture is a benefit that you can pitch to potential clients.

Instructions—Visit the American Society for Horticultural Science site to find out which schools offer a degree in horticulture and get a degree or certificate.

Contact your government center for business license information. Register your business name and get any necessary permits.

Apply for a business loan so you can buy your tree trimming equipment. You will need to start with a truck, tree saws, circular saws, chainsaws, handsaws, ladders, harnesses, ropes, hand pruners, landscaping shears and loppers. Write out your budget before you apply for a loan. Most tree trimming services require $10,000-$50,000 in startup capital.

Hire tree trimmer workers and train them in your methods. You can advertise online or hire people through a labor workforce agency.

Team up with companies that work in lawn care and offer discounts to gain potential customers.

Tips & Warnings—Focus on getting government and business contracts because they pay more than residential. Your workers should be insured and have workman's comp due to the dangerous nature of this business.

Horticulture and Allied Sectors

'Horticulture and allied' sector is an integral element for food and nutritional security in the country. Horticulture is the main segment, while its various sub-segments are fruits, vegetables, aromatic and herbal plants, flowers, spices and plantation crops. All these are regarded as the essential ingredients of economic security. The wide range of agro-climatic conditions of India is conducive for growing a large variety of horticultural crops, including, root and tuber crops, mushroom, ornamental crops, plantation crops like coconut, arecanut, cashew and cocoa.

The Government of India has recognized horticulture crops as a means of diversification in agriculture in an eco-friendly manner through efficient use of land and optimum utilization of natural resources. Horticulture seeks to create ample opportunities for employment, particularly for unemployed youths and women folk. India has maintained leadership in the production of many commodities like mango, banana, acid lime, coconut, arecanut, cashew, ginger, turmeric and black pepper. Presently, it is the second largest producer of fruits and vegetables in the world.

India is next only to China in area and production of vegetables and occupies prime position in the production of cauliflower, second in onions and third in cabbage in the world. India has also made noticeable advancement in the production of flowers. Further, it is the largest producer, consumer and exporter of spices. India is home to a wide variety of spices like black pepper, cardamom (small and large), ginger, garlic, turmeric, chilli and a large variety of tree and seed spices. Almost all the States in the country grow one or more spices. The major spice producing States are Andhra Pradesh, Tamil Nadu, Orissa and Madhya Pradesh. North Eastern region and Andaman and Nicobar Islands also have potential areas cultivated for spices, particularly organically.

Further, coconut is a versatile crop and about 10 million people depend on its cultivation, processing and related activities. It is grown mainly along the coastal States of the country as well as in the North-Eastern region. It is grown over an area of 1.84 million ha with a production of 8.67 million tonnes. India is a leading country in the world for coconut production.

Thus, over the years, much progress has been made for the advancement of horticulture and allied sector. Rising investments have resulted in increased production and availability of horticultural produce in the rural and urban areas. Many schemes and policies have been introduced, from time to time, for upliftment and commercialisation of the sector. Large number of investors are taking advantage of the existing potentials in the sector, as well as trying to explore the untapped potentials.

CASE STUDY

The American Boxwood Society

The Society's headquarters is at the State Arboretum of Virginia, formerly the University of Virginia's Orland E. White Arboretum, at Blandy Experimental Farm, Clarke County, Virginia. There the ABS has established and currently supports the ABS Memorial Garden, developed as a memorial to two early leaders of the Society, who died in 1974, Henry Hohman of the Kingsville Nursery, Maryland and Dr. John T. Baldwin of the College of William and Mary, Williamsburg, VA. The Memorial Garden now includes over 100 different species and varieties, all labeled. The ABS also serves as the International Registration Authority for cultivated *Buxus* L. It sponsors and partially funds scientific research projects on *Buxus*. The ABS is dedicated to making popular the use of boxwood in landscapes throughout the country.

Central Virginia Nursery & Landscape Association

In order to help our members maintain the highest level of current knowledge and professionalism, we hold monthly dinner meetings with educational speakers; sponsor a special three-day "Short Course" the first of each year, providing our members with up-to-date horticultural information on both basic and technical subjects; and sponsor a Certification Study Program to help our members prepare for the Virginia Certified Professional exams.

The CVNLA supports funding of horticultural research and provides information to home owners at events such as the Maymont Flower & Garden Show, (where our exhibits have won ribbons for its quality and educational message!) the Virginia State Fair, the Virginia Green Industry Council's Virginia Garden Festival, and Earth Day.

Remember that a "bargain" tree that turns brown two months after planting isn't a bargain, no matter how little it cost! So when it's time for that creative solution for your home or business landscape - that maximizes your landscape dollars - refer to our Member Business Directory to locate a professional that will help you develop a personal and unique solution ...one that is designed for your lifestyle, your budget, and your light and soil conditions.

Claybrooke Farm

Celebrating the real experiences of the season begins with the journey to the field and the quest for the perfect Christmas tree. Claybrooke Farm takes pride in offering the setting for this all important family tradition. It is our hope that we can help you experience a little of that holiday tradition by visiting with us at our farm.

Each year many families visit our farm to select their Christmas tree. We have thousands of trees from which to choose and do our best to ensure customer satisfaction. We cater to families and the elderly by providing close parking, well maintained fields and courteous service. We have reasonable prices and strive to provide a quality tree for every budget!

Claybrooke Farm planted his first Christmas trees in 1984 when it was expecting its first child. With that act and the desire to diversify family income it was anticipating a way to pay for future college expenses for not just one, but two sons, Matthew and Tyler. It has planted thousands of seedlings since that time.

This now offer five different species for harvest andhave grown our operation to over 15,000 trees. Currently, It is in the process of expanding the operation to offer even more variety including a small container nursery. With now two foresters in the family, It manage all of our farm and forest land in an environmentally friendly sustainable manner. Claybrooke is home to a diverse array of wildlife, including deer, geese, bear,turkey, quail, rabbit, fox, bald eagle, and song birds. Upon your visit to Claybrooke; you might have the opportunity to observe some of these species.

It has a rich history dating back to 1725 when it was a Land Grant to the Overton family. The property was named "Brookeville" and was passed to the Claybrooke family through marriage. John Claybrooke was quite an entrepreneur and became well established in the community. He supplied ties for the railroad at Frederick Hall during the Civil War. Most of the land was open at that time providing acreage for cattle, sheep, corn, hay, hogs, and tobacco. Members of the Overton and Claybrooke families are buried on the property.

Those early families probably celebrated the holiday with a red cedar Christmas tree cut from the farm. The farm came to us through Virginia's family in 1982.

When Virginia and her two sisters were small, Claybrooke was primarily a cattle and crop operation, boasting not just cattle and crops, but a few pigs, chickens, dogs, cats, as well as garden vegetables and flowers. Respecting the farm's history and realizing that we are only temporary stewards of this beautiful land, we chose to keep the property named "Claybrooke" in honor of the ones who toiled here before us.

Duis Nursery

Founded by William H. Duis in 1952, we cater to landscapers and garden centers and we pride ourselves in the high-quality of our products. We grow a wide range of plants in order to provide our customers with many choices in their design applications. Furthermore, we have begun to "re-wholesale" items that we do not grow or that are temporarily out of stock.

All of our plants are selected for their hardiness. As you study our pricelist, you will see that we grow a selection of evergreens and flowering shrubs that will withstand even the harshest Virginia winters. And we specialize in those hollies and azaleas that have been especially bred for Zones 5 and 6. We are again growing hardy Camellias that will thrive in Piedmont Virginia if properly located in the landscape.

Our trees are grown in "pot-in-pot" systems that allow us to harvest them 365 days a year with no transplant shock. And our perennials, grown in one gallon containers, are fully over-wintered in cold houses or outside and are ready for the landscape.

If there are plants that you like that you do not see in our price list, let us know and perhaps we can begin to grow them.

CHAPTER–4

TRADE SHOWS, EXHIBITIONS AND FAIR FOR HORTICULTURAL TOURISM

AMERICAN ROYAL

The American Royal in Kansas City, Missouri is a livestock show, horse show and rodeo held each year in October and November at Kemper Arena. The Future Farmers of America was founded during the Royal and Kansas City's professional baseball team the Kansas City Royals derive their name from the Royal.

The American Royal began as a cattle show in 1899 in the Kansas City Stockyards. The name "American Royal" was inspired by a 1901 editorial in beef industry publication Kansas City Drovers Telegram entitled "Call It The American Royal." The editorial noted the Royal Agricultural Society in England has a similar event called the Royal Show.

The first American Royal horse show was added in 1907, and has grown to include five shows (Quarter Horse, Hunter-Jumper Horse, Arabian Horses, American Saddlebred and a 4-H show).

In 1926, the American Royal invited vocational agriculture students to judge livestock. During the 1928 American Royal, 33 of the students meeting at the Baltimore Hotel in downtown Kansas City formed the Future Farmers of America. The group proceeded to hold a convention every year during the Royal in Kansas City until 1998.

The original home of the American Royal was destroyed by fire on Valentines Day in 1925. The structure was rebuilt in time for the event that year and served as the center for events until the American Royal complex was built across from Kemper Arena in 1992. During World War II, the Royal complex was converted into a glider factory.

The American Royal is an annual eight-week season of barbecue competition, rodeos, livestock shows, equestrian events and agricultural activities benefiting youth and education. The barbecue contest is divided into several categories: brisket, pork ribs, pork shoulder, chicken, sausage, side dishes and dessert.

The American Royal, one of Kansas City's premier fall events with annual economic impact of more than $62 million, hosts the world's largest barbecue contest, one of the Midwest's largest livestock exhibitions, one of the top five ranked rodeos in the nation and is home of the national championship horse competition.

The American Royal is a not-for-profit, community volunteer-based service organization which raises funds to fulfill its vision & mission through endowments contributions, sponsorships and event revenues.

In 2005, the organization contributed more than $1.3 million in financial support in the form of scholarships, educational awards, educational programs, community donations, competitive awards and prize monies and premiums.

Clay County Fair

The Clay County Fair is held every September in Spencer, Iowa. It is the largest county fair in the state of Iowa. It has the second largest agricultural exposition in North America. Bringing in over 310,000 visitors a year, the Clay County Fair is one of the largest county fairs in the United States. Beginning in 1918, the fair has grown considerably over the past near century.

In its first year the Clay County Fair brought in 30,000 guests. In 1936 the fair completed the construction of its second grandstand, able to seat over 7,500 people, which it still uses today. During the 1930s the fair continued construction of agricultural buildings for livestock. The Clay County Fair has firmly planted itself as the largest Midwest county fair.

The fair also hosts a carnival of over 80 rides and attractions. There are also many businesses that have booths all over the fair. It consists of over 3 city blocks of space, and continues to fill up the space tighter and tighter every year.

Some familiar people/groups who have visited and/or performed at the Clay County Fair are: President George W. Bush, Sen. John Kerry, former Vice President Al Gore, Bob Hope, Lynyrd Skynyrd, Johnny Cash, Tim McGraw, Kenny Rogers, LeeAnn Womack, Martina McBride, REO Speedwagon, The Righteous Brothers, Plus One, Clay Aiken, ZZ Top, LeAnn Rimes, Brad Paisley, Lee Greenwood, Bill Cosby, Red Skelton, Jim Nabors, Lonestar, Grand Funk Railroad, Garth Brooks, Survivor, Trisha Yearwood, Heart and Foreigner. On September 15, 2007 Aly and AJ played there for the first time in Iowa.

With the completion of the Clay County Regional Events Center inside the fairground walls, new opportunities have opened. Some of these are indoor concerts. With seating up to 3,400 people, the events center has hosted The Barnum and Bailey Circus, and the Lipizzan Stallions. It also has a large ballroom/dining room capable of seating up to 400 people, just creating even more opportunities to flourish and grow.

The Fair has just completed another project in 2007. The Race Track was modified into a 3/8 track. The previous track was a large, flat, half-mile oval that was generally used for horse racing. In order to host high-quality auto racing events, the fair deemed it necessary to construct a completely new racetrack. It was converted to a 3/8 mile clay track, with increased corner banking to adjust for the higher speeds of auto racing. Additionally, a state-of-the-art lighting system was installed to make the races more visible for both drivers and fans.

In 2008, the racing schedule featured the International Motor Contest Association (IMCA) hosting two classes of racing; Modifieds and Stock Cars. Those races also included Hobby Stocks and 360 Modifieds. July 4th, the WorldDirt Racing League (WDRL) also hosted a Late Model Series and 360 Sprints on the track. The season rounded out with an appearance by the World of Outlaws during the 2008 Clay County Fair and another race with IMCA Modifieds and Stock Cars, with Hobby Stocks and 360 Modifieds.

FARM PROGRESS SHOW

In 1953, Prairie Farmer teamed with WLS Radio in Chicago to host a field day where farmers could see first-hand the progress being made in farming equipment, along with seed varieties and ag chemicals.

In subsequent years, the show evolved to include seed test plots and field demonstrations. The show typically was held annually at different sites in Illinois, Iowa, and Indiana. As the event grew, it became apparent that temporary sites were inadequate to handle the large crowds and exhibits.

The Farm Progress Show is the U.S.' largest outdoor farm show. In 2005, a permanent biennial exhibit site was constructed near Decatur, Illinois which hosted its inaugural show in 2005. For the 2007 show, the site was expanded and upgraded with asphalt paved streets. The Decatur site is one of two permanent biennial sites constructed to host the show. Boone, Iowa, was selected for the show's second permanent biennial site. In 2008 the show site hosted its first show at its newly constructed permanent biennial facility. The show now alternates between these two permanent sites on an annual basis.

The Boone site is developed on about 600 acres (2.4 km2) at the intersection of U.S. Highway 30 and Iowa Highway 17, while the Decatur show site includes 640 acres (2.6 km2) of exhibits and field demonstrations.

The Farm Progress Show is the oldest and largest outdoor agricultural equipment exhibition in the United States with more than 500 exhibitors. Farm Progress Companies does not release attendance figures, but the Decatur Convention & Visitors Bureau estimates attendance of at least 150,000 for the three days of the 2007 show.

In 1959 ABC Broadcasting/Paramount Theaters bought the Farm Progress Group - Prairie Farmer, Wallaces Farmer and the Wisconsin Agriculturist.

In 1986 ABC merged with Capital Cities and in 1996 the Disney Company purchased Capital Cities/ABC. In 1997, the Disney Company sold the Farm Progress Companies to Rural Press. Rural Press merged with Fairfax in 2007.

Farm Progress Companies is owned by Fairfax Media, an Australian media company based in New South Wales.

Southwestern Exposition and Livestock Show

The Southwestern Exposition and Livestock Show, known commonly as the Fort Worth Stock Show and Rodeo is the oldest continual running livestock show and rodeo. It has been held annually in Fort Worth, Texas since 1896. In 1918, the Stock Show held the world's first indoor rodeo, and in subsequent years has been responsible for several milestones in the sport of rodeo. A non-profit organization, the Stock Show provided over $1.6 million in grants and scholarships from 2000 to 2006.

The city of Fort Worth was nicknamed "Cowtown" shortly after the Civil War, as cowboys stopped for supplies in the town while herding their cattle from South Texas to the Chisholm Trail. After the arrival of the Texas and Pacific Railway in 1876, various businesspeople in the town began erecting stock yards in an effort to become a greater part of the cattle industry. In 1883, the Fort Worth Stockyards were official incorporated.

Local ranchers wished to facilitate interest in their cattle. A conversation between rancher Charles McFarland and Charles French, marketing manager for the Fort Worth Stock Yards, resulted in the first area stock show in 1896. This event was the first of what would eventually become known as the Southwestern Exposition and Livestock Show. The stock show was held along Marine Creek, in a location with no buildings or enclosures, and only a few trees to provide shade for the animals and patrons. Early–day cattle exhibitors and organizers were all Texans: Capt. William S. Ikard of Henrietta, a breeder of Herefords; I. K. Kimberlin of Sherman; Col. J. W. Burgess of Fort Worth, a Shorthorn breeder, and Col. B. C. Rhome of Denton and Wise Counties. These men were joined enthusiastically by operators of the Fort Worth Stock Yards Company, which was organized in 1893; Armour & Company and Swift & Company, meat packers; and officials of the various railway companies serving Fort Worth.

That first show was such a success that organizers gathered again in the fall of 1896 for a two-day event in October to coincide with the National Livestock Exchange Convention meeting. A parade opened the fall show. Most exhibitors preferred the spring dates, so the Show was established as a March event, to fit in with a series of major livestock shows held around the country, establishing a regular circuit for exhibitor herds.

The following year, the event was given a name, the Texas Fat Stock Show. Tents were erected for the animals, and visitors were charged a twenty-five cent fee to view the livestock.

Local ranchers promoted the show to northern meat packers in the hopes of improving the local livestock industry. The citizens of Fort Worth raised $50,000 and formed a company in 1904 to oversee the event. Under the group's second president, Samuel Burk Burnett, the annual show was renamed the Southwestern Exposition and Fat Stock Show. During his term, which lasted from 1908-1922, the event dramatically expanded. The North Side Coliseum (now called Cowtown Coliseum) was built in 1908 to house the event. The new indoor judging arena created expanded interest in the Stock Show, and a carnival and midway were soon added. Commercial exhibit displays also increased in number, and exhibitors travelled from several surrounding states to participate.

Houston Livestock Show and Rodeo

The Houston Livestock Show and Rodeo, also called RodeoHouston, is the world's largest livestock exhibition as well as the richest regular-season PRCA rodeo event, held at Reliant Park in Houston, Texas, USA. In 2010, attendance reached a record high of 2.2 million , requiring more than 22,000 volunteers. In 2007, the Rodeo was deemed "the year of the volunteer." The event is 20 days long. It is kicked off by the Downtown Rodeo Roundup held near Houston City Hall, the Downtown Rodeo parade and the ConocoPhillips Rodeo Run - 5k walk & run and the World's Championship Bar-B-Que Contest. The Show features championship Rodeo action including bull riding, livestock judging, concerts, a carnival, pig racing, barbecue and the Rodeo Uncorked! International Wine Competition, shopping, sales and livestock auctions. Traditional trail rides, which start in different areas of Texas and end in Houston, precede the Rodeo events. . The City of Houston celebrates this event with Go Texan Days, where residents are encouraged to dress in western wear for the duration of the Show.

The rodeo has drawn some of the world's biggest stars and music legends, including Elvis Presley, Bob Dylan, Brooks & Dunn, George Strait, Reba McEntire, Garth Brooks, Willie Nelson, Selena, ZZ Top & Lynyrd Skynyrd, among others.

The wide variety of entertainment at The Houston Livestock Show and Rodeo has proven to be a popular feature of the event, as it caters to a multitude of tastes. Previous performers include country, rock, blues, Tejano, and pop musicians, stand-up comedians, and even actors.

With a daily average attendance of the Rodeo of about 50,000 people, the city's transportation infrastructure is taxed as it must also compete with regular Houston Rush Hour on regular business days. There are a variety of ways into and out of the complex that include Park and Ride lots in certain parts of the city that are provided by the event as an express straight onto the property, Taxi, Self Parking, and METRORail. The Coordinators of the event try to persuade attendees to use public transportation as the most convenient way to and from the Rodeo.

National Farm Machinery Show

The National Farm Machinery Show is recognized as one of the largest indoor farm machinery expositions in the United States. The show is typically held annually in February at the Kentucky Exposition Center in Louisville, Kentucky. Attendance exceeds 300,000 people, with 800 exhibitors in display space of 1,200,000 square feet (111,000 m2).

This massive show features thousands of widely recognized agricultural products and services showcased by more than 800 exhibitors in 1,200,000 square feet (111,000 m2) of interconnected exhibit space.

The National Farm Machinery Show boasts the nation's oldest tractor pull, Championship Tractor Pull. Officially introduced to the world in 1969 during the fourth National Farm Machinery Show (NFMS), the Championship Tractor Pull is now celebrating 40 years of making champions. The competition had been a vision of its originator, Billy Joe Miles, and was so popular in its first year that 15 drivers signed up to compete in the inaugural pull before it was officially established. Popularity can also be due to world-class tractors who participate, such as Silver Bullet, an AGCO White.

Today the pull remains a counterpart to the much larger NFMS, but the CTP has since transformed into a premiere event of its own. For 40 years, Freedom's Hall's basketball court has converted into a championship dirt track to showcase some of the nation's best drivers in fierce pulling competition. Each year, a short list of pullers etch their names in history as they become part of an elite group of drivers earning a national championship title. CTP brings in more than 75,000 fans to watch five performances in four days.

The exposition produces an estimated economic impact of $21.5 million each year, the most of any event held at the Kentucky Exposition Center.

Pennsylvania Farm Show

The Pennsylvania Farm Show is held every January at the Pennsylvania Farm Show Complex & Expo Center located in Harrisburg, Pennsylvania, just off Exit 67 of Interstate 81. The event, considered Pennsylvania's state fair, first began in 1917. It is the largest indoor agricultural event held in the United States. The Farm Show Complex houses 24 acres under roof, spread throughout 11 buildings including three arenas. The annual event is free to the public and attracts over half a million visitors. The Sheep to Shawl Competition was added to the show in 2008.

Royal Show

The Royal Show was an annual agricultural show/fair held by the Royal Agricultural Society of England every year from 1839 to 2009. It was held in Stoneleigh Park (previously known as the National Agricultural Centre or NAC) near Stoneleigh in Warwickshire, England. Early venues for the show included Park Royal in London and Victoria Park, Leamington Spa.

The event encompassed all aspects of farming, food and rural life - from the best of British livestock to the latest business and technological innovations in the farming industry. Over 1,000 stands, world-class lifestock and equine classes attracted visitors from over 100 countries.

On 3 April 2009, organisers said the 2009 show would be the last.

Royal Show 2007

More than 140,000 visitors were expected to attend the 2007 show; however, bad weather forced the show to close early for the first time in its history. Torrential rains left the showground saturated and police and show organisers took the decision to close the show a day ahead of schedule "to ensure the safety and welfare of the public, traders and exhibitors".

Two of the showground's car parks were closed on Monday evening after drivers had to be towed free. A further 30 acres (12 ha) of barley and hay fields were mowed to provide additional parking on the Tuesday.

The decision was described as "heartbreaking" by the Royal Agricultural Society of England. John Moverley, RASE Chief Executive, said the financial implications of the wet weather and closing the show early were being assessed. "We haven't got exact figures, but it looks as though we are down by about 10% for the first two days on last year," he said.

ROYAL HIGHLAND SHOW

The Royal Highland Show is Scotland's annual farming and countryside showcase. It is held annually at the Royal

Highland Centre, Ingliston over the second-last weekend in June (Thursday - Sunday), the event attracts over 1,000 exhibitors, 4,500 head of livestock, and an annual 150,000 visitors - making it Scotland's most popular summer event and the premier fixture in Scotland's farming calendar. It generates over £200 million in business . Exhibitors compete for the prestige of winning not only a prize ticket, but also for prize money and trophies worth over £1 million. It is the UK's largest agricultural event and the longest lasting one sponsored by new holland .

Royal Norfolk Show

The Royal Norfolk Show is an annual agricultural show, and is held by the Royal Norfolk Agricultural Association. It is the largest 2 day agricultural show in England, and has been held almost every year since 1847. Shows were not held in 1866, 1911, 1934 and 1957. Up until 1953, the show was held at various sites around Norfolk, although it has since been held at a permanent site near Costessey, Norwich, Norfolk. The show tends to be held on the Wednesday and Thursday in week 26 of the year.

Royal Welsh Show

The Royal Welsh Show (Welsh: Sioe Frenhinol Cymru) is the biggest agricultural show in Europe. It is organised by the Royal Welsh Agricultural Society, which was formed in 1904, and takes place in July of each year, at Llanelwedd, near Builth Wells, in Powys, Mid Wales.

The first show was held in Aberystwyth in 1904, and its success led to the development of the permanent showground at Llanelwedd, first used in 1963.

Royal Cornwall Show

The Royal Cornwall Agricultural Show, usually called the Royal Cornwall Show, is an agricultural show organised by the The Royal Cornwall Agricultural Association, which takes place at the beginning of June each year, at Wadebridge in North Cornwall.

The show lasts for three days and attracts approximately 120,000 visitors annually, making it one of Cornwall's major tourist attractions.

Tendring Hundred Show

Tendring Hundred Show is an annual agricultural fair held in early July at the Showground at Lawford House Park, near Manningtree in Essex England, featuring over 200 tradestands and entertainment in several show areas and shows.

East of England Agricultural Society

The East of England Agricultural Society in the United Kingdom is the organiser of the East of England Show held each year at the 250 acre (101 ha) East of England Showground, five miles (8 km) west of the city of Peterborough in Cambridgeshire.

The Society was formed by the merger of the Cambridgeshire and Isle of Ely (established 1863), Huntingdonshire (established 1837) and Peterborough (established 1797) agricultural societies in 1970. It was joined by the Bedfordshire Agricultural Society (1801) in 1971 and the Northamptonshire Agricultural Society (1848) in 1972. The Long Sutton Agricultural Society (1837) in neighbouring Lincolnshire remains independent and is affiliated for show purposes only.

Great Yorkshire Show

The Great Yorkshire Show (GYS) is an agricultural show which takes place on the Great Yorkshire Showground in Harrogate, North Yorkshire in the North of England annually from the second Tuesday of July until the following Thursday. It is organised and run by the Yorkshire Agricultural Society (YAS).

The history of the GYS is intimately connected with that of the Yorkshire Agricultural Society (YAS). At its foundation in 1837, the primary aim of the YAS was stated as "... to hold an Annual Meeting for the Exhibition of Farming Stock, Implements &c., and for the General Promotion of Agriculture."

The first YAS Show was held in 1838 in the Barrack Yard at Fulford, near York. Though the numbers attending were not recorded the event was counted a success; police had to use their truncheons to restore order among the large numbers of visitors when they began to force their way in without paying .

Originally intended as a peripatetic event, the Show moved to Leeds, Northallerton and Hull in subsequent years, before returning to York in 1842. This is the first year for which attendance figures are available — the Show in 1842 had a paid attendance of 6044 . By 1843 the YAS Show had become known as the "Great Yorkshire Show", apparently by popular acclamation rather than in any official sense.

The GYS continued to be held in various places around Yorkshire until 1950. No GYS was held between 1915-1919 due to World War I while the 1920 GYS was held jointly with the RASE in Darlington. Shows between 1940-1948 were cancelled due to World War II. By 1948 the YAS was coming to the conclusion that the expenses involved in setting up a new showground every year were becoming prohibitive , and in 1949 it was decided that a permanent showground be acquired. In 1950 the last of the peripatetic shows was held in Malton.

In 1950 the YAS purchased a site at Hook Oval in Harrogate for the sum of £16,500, and since 1951 this has been the permanent site for the GYS. In 1951 the attendance figure was nearly 54,000.

The 2001 GYS was cancelled due to the outbreak of Foot and mouth disease in Britain.

The 2006 show has been the most successful so far in terms of attendance figures, with 135,111 visitors.

The 2008 show was attended by the Queen to celebrate its 150th anniversary.

Monmouth Show

The Monmouth Show is the largest one-day agricultural show in Wales, taking place annually in Monmouth. The origins of the show date back to the 1790s when the town's agricultural society organised ploughing matches. Another landmark event was on May 30th, 1857, when the eighth Duke of Beaufort and Sir Charles Morgan M.P. each put £10 into a fund to start the Monmouth Cattle Show.

The modern origins of the show date to 1875 when a show was held in the town's newly established cattle market in Chippenham Fields. The show was then held annually (firstly in October, but then eventually moved to August - taking up its now traditional date of the last Thursday in August) up until the First World War. The show was restarted in 1919 when it was renamed the Monmouthshire County Show. The show was not held during the period of the Second World War, but from 1946 until 2006 it was held each year on the grounds of Vauxhall Fields. The show was not held in 1956 or 2001 due to outbreaks of foot and mouth disease. 2007 marked the 150th anniversary of the Monmouthshire Show Society. That same year the show moved to a new site on the Redbrook Road in Monmouth.

Newport Show

Newport Show is held at Chetwynd Park show ground at Chetwynd, Shropshire, England, between Newport and Edgmond. The show can trace its roots back to 1890, when a group of local farmers joined to become Newport and District Agricultural Society.

Friday, August 8, 1890 was the date of the first show, which was held at Victoria Park. A schedule of classes was drawn up to include livestock, root crops, implements, cheese, butter, wool, horse leaping and turnouts. There was even a prize for male and female servants of Society members.

Thus the Newport and District Agricultural Society was founded, to organise the annual Newport Show and for the improvement of agriculture. To this day, it bears all of the hallmarks of that early tradition and is acknowledged as the best one day show in the Midlands . The show still keeps strong ties with the town and the town's educational establishments, especially Harper Adams University College.

New Forest Show

The New Forest and Hampshire County Show, or more commonly known as "The New Forest Show" is an annual agricultural show event held for three days at the end of July in New Park, near Brockenhurst in Hampshire, southern England, UK.

The show attracts over 100,000 visitors every year, and brings together a celebration of traditional country pursuits, crafts, produce and entertainment. Show jumping is another major feature at the show and there are competitive classes throughout all three days. A full range of equestrian classes also features, as well as livestock competitions including pigs, cattle and sheep, plus a poultry section, rabbits, cage birds, and honey bees.

The first New Forest Show was in 1921, and in 2006, it celebrated its 80th show. The show is also great for local business as well as agricultural business, food, flowers and vegetable displays bringing together all aspects of rural life.

Shropshire and West Midlands Show

The Shropshire and West Midlands Show, though usually called the West Mid Show, is an annual agriculture-related show held on the outskirts of Shrewsbury (at Coton Hill), England.

It has its own showground - the Shropshire Agricultural Showground, which lies on the north bank of the River Severn in a rural setting (though it is also only a mile from Shrewsbury town centre). The showground is accessed via Berwick Road, the B5067.

The show is held usually in May and attracts as many as 40,000 people, from across the region.

On 07 November 2009 the society which runs the show went into liquidation, all staff were made redundant with immediate effect. . Shropshire County Council have taken over as organisers, and the event has been renamed the Shropshire County Show.

International Agri & Flora Tech (IAFT)

International Agri & Flora Tech (IAFT) 2010, one of the most innovative agriculture technology exhibition scheduled from 3rd to 6th September 2010, Palace Grounds, Bangalore, INDIA. IAFT 2010 is an International exhibition on Agriculture and Horticulture Technologies which will not only give the visitors an insight into the benefits of the new technology, but also provide them an opportunity to interact with the exhibitors. It will be an meeting ground for inputs, supports & service from all over the world to find business opportunities in a competitive environment and provides a opportunity to facilitate business deals for agriculture products and equipment under one roof.

International Agri & Flora Tech 2010 is going to pump new technologies and advances in agriculture and horticulture practices. The event will be an eye-opener to the growers and other stakeholders of every segment of Agriculture and allied activities who want to expand and diversify their activities in the industry.

International Agri & Flora Tech 2010 offers unparalleled networking opportunity and brings decision makers and opinion leaders in Agriculture on a common platform to exchange ideas and explore new business opportunities.

Krishi Mahotsav

Krishi Mahotsav is the first in the country arranging Focused, Local Need based events for the farmers. The main objective for organizing this Expo is to exhibit/highlight the latest agricultural technologies developed in the country and policies and programmes of the Ministry of Agriculture, Government of India for the benefit of the visitors who would include farmers, scientists, extension professionals and general public.

Kisan Expo

KISAN 2010 will be the 18th event in KISAN series. KISAN is Indias Largest show in agriculture, Its is the 18th event in the successful KISAN Series, Brings Decision Makers and Opinion Leaders in Agriculture on a common platform. KISAN Series is striving to bring every farmer face to face with the advanced technologies & innovations in the agriculture.

India International Tea & Coffee Expo

India International Tea & Coffee Expo(IITCE)-2010 is an unique three day exhibition for Tea & Coffee products. This exhibition will be designed for Tea, Coffee, Machinery allied services and supplier to reach their targeted customer and ease the visitors to find their particular needs. India International Tea & Coffee Expo (IITCE) is only exclusive show in India where all leading Tea & Coffee company will showcase their products.

Royal Agricultural Winter Fair (Canada)

The Royal Agricultural Winter Fair, colloquially called The Royal, is an annual fall fair in Toronto, Ontario, Canada, which takes place over two weeks in November. Inaugurated in 1922, and originally housed in the Coliseum, on the grounds of Exhibition Place, the event has expanded to also take up the Direct Energy National Trade Centre, and remains an important exhibit for livestock breeders. Elizabeth II, as Queen of Canada, is the fair's royal patron.

ROYAL NEW ZEALAND SHOW

The Royal New Zealand Show, first held in 1924, is an annual agricultural show held by the Royal Agricultural Society of New Zealand, an umbrella organization for agricultural and pastoral associations in New Zealand. The show was formerly held in rotation at Palmerston North, Hawke's Bay, Hamilton, Invercargill and Christchurch. Starting in 2006, the show was hosted by the Canterbury Agricultural and Pastoral Association at Canterbury Agricultural Park in Christchurch; this ended in 2010, inclusive.

Cloone Agricultural Show (Ireland)

On August Bank Holiday Monday Cloone's Annual Agricultural Show will take place in the Show Grounds on the Ballinamore road. Since its inception in 1988 Cloone show has grown to become one of the premier agriculture shows in the west of Ireland.

With its huge variety of classes and attractions there is sure to be something for everyone at this years show. At Cloone Show you will see rural Ireland showcased in the most traditional way in the picturesque surroundings of Co. Leitrim.

Castlerea Agricultural Trade & Craft Show (Ireland)

The Castlerea Agricultural Trade & Craft Show committee is currently preparing for our 2010 Show which will take place on Bank Holiday Monday, August 2nd 2010. Once again our main sponsor is Cahill's SuperValu. Proprietor Anthony Cahill was one of the core organizing committee members when the Show was reintroduced in1995 after a lapse of many years and has remained a loyal supporter since then.

La Rural (Argentina)

La Exposición Rural (in English: The Rural Exhibition), is an annual agricultural and livestock show held in the Palermo section of Buenos Aires, Argentina. The event is organised by La Sociedad Rural Argentina (in English: The Argentine Rural Society) and both the Exhibition and the Society are known locally as La Rural.

The exhibition has taken place in the society's Santa Fe Avenue exhibition centre and fairground, each year in July since 1886. Primarily a farming show, breeders arrive from all over the country to exhibit their livestock, particularly cattle. It became a major feature of the porteño social scene in prosperous Argentina, taking place in Buenos Aires' most exclusive neighbourhood and accompanied by balls and other events. However, with the onset of the country's economic crisis towards the end of the 20th century, the event lost some of its vitality, although it is still popular with visitors. In 2005, 715,000 people visited the exhibition, which had almost 400 stands and 4,000 animals.

The Society was founded on 10 July 1866 by Eduardo Olivera and José Martínez de Hoz with the motto 'To cultivate the soil is to serve the country', and was formally known as 'El Solar de Palermo'. Built in the 1870s, the Society's showground features a Belle Epoque stadium and a modern exhibition hall. During the rest of the year, the exhibition hall is used for other events including trade shows. The Opera Pampa organises shows in the stadium, showcasing the history of Argentina with zamba dances and an asado in the dining rooms. With over 10,000 members, the Society has branch offices in many parts of the country.

Expointer (Brazil)

Expointer is an agricultural show with national importance in Brazil that occurs every year in the Parque de

Exposições Assis Brasil in the city of Esteio, in the metropolitan area of Porto Alegre in the brazilian state of Rio Grande do Sul. It is considered the largest livestock show in Latin America. The first edition occurred on february 24 in 1901, in Porto Alegre. In 2004 the fair received a record public of 720 thousand people.

Paris International Agricultural Show (France)

Paris International Agricultural Show is one of the world's largest and most important agricultural shows, drawing larger crowds than any other exposition in Paris except the Foire de Paris. This annual fair takes place end of February or beginning of March at the Porte de Versailles in Paris, France. This event was first held in 1870 as the Concours général agricole, its name changed in 1964 , but the Concours still exists and is one of the main attractions of the fair.

ROYAL HORTICULTURAL HALLS

Royal Horticultural Halls & Conference Centre is a multipurpose venue of Westminster. With two elegant and historic halls popular for corporate banquets, product launches and exhibitions this has been the perfect venue. The conference centre is known for offering the best daily delegate rate in the town. Royal Horticultural Halls & Conference Centre boasts of its multifunctional and flexible areas and of its capability to host different kinds of events. Thousands of visitors, organizer and exhibitor gather at the exhibition center to take the advantage of functional and flexible spaces build for them. This venue provides catering service and conferences and events for up to 1800 guests can be hosted here.

Chapter–5

HORTICULTURAL TOURIST ATTRACTION

PLEASURE BEACH

Pleasure Beach, Blackpool formerly 'Blackpool Pleasure Beach' is a family owned amusement park and resort situated along the Fylde coast in Blackpool, England. It is the most visited amusement park in the United Kingdom, and one of the top twenty most-visited amusement parks in the world with 5.5 million visitors in 2007 . In 2003 the park became an official resort following the opening of the Big Blue Hotel which was founded the same year. The park is a privately funded business and is owned, managed and directed by the Thompson family.

The park was initially founded in 1896 by William George Bean after he failed in his attempt to become an advertising man on New York's Madison Avenue. He returned to the UK in 1897 and opened two separate amusement parks; one adjacent to Euston Road in Great Yarmouth and another in Blackpool. The Yarmouth amusement park consisted simply of a switchback railway and bicycle railway called the Hotchkiss's Patented Railroad. Bean stayed in Yarmouth until the end of the century before moving to Blackpool full time.

In 1903 Bean, along with businessman John Outhwaite, purchased 30 acres of land known as the "Watson Estate" to be rented out by various trade stalls and traditional fairground rides and in 1905 the name "Blackpool Pleasure Beach" was chosen. In 1910, Blackpool Pleasure Beach LTD was founded by Bean and Outhwaite, and to this day remains the name of the company which the Thompson family uses to manage the park. Outhwaite died in 1911, leaving the initial business to Bean, however the Outhwaite family still had ownership in shares of the park. Further investment included the building of The Casino, The Whip, Virginia Reel, Noah's Ark, Big Dipper and Dodgems.

In 1923 land was reclaimed from the sea front. It was at this period that the park moved to its 44 acre current location above what became Watson Road, which was built under the Pleasure Beach in 1932. In 1929 Bean died suddenly of pneumonia leaving the park to his daughter, Lillian 'Doris' Bean, who had previously married a young businessman, Leonard Thompson, in 1928. Thompson was an Oxford natural sciences graduate who after Bean's death immediately took over the Pleasure Beach with his wife. The park came under full control of the Thompson family after the remaining Outhwaite family sold their share of the park. Leonard Thompson became the managing director and Lillian Dorris, who later became known as Mrs L.D Thompson, OBE, became a secondary manager and director. The couple had a son named Geoffrey.

In 1976 Leonard Thompson died unexpectedly and six months later the company secretary also died suddenly, leaving Doris Thompson commercially in charge of the whole business. Appointed chairman; she gave the role of managing director to her eldest son, Geoffrey. He had previously administered the New Era Laundries in London before returning to the Pleasure Beach as head of catering at the Casino Building. He married his wife, Barbara, shortly afterwards and they had three children, Amanda, Nicholas and Fiona. After Leonard's death, Geoffrey and his mother steadily extended the Pleasure Beach business, opening both Pleasureland Southport and Frontierland, Morecambe and invested into food-and-ride trade at the Pleasure Beach. He saw the opening of the Steeplechase, Avalanche, Revolution (now Irn-Bru Revolution), Pepsi Max Big One, PlayStation: The Ride! (now Tango Ice Blast: The Ride) and Valhalla.

He also became a world wide figure in the tourism industry and was involved in promoting tourism nationally. He sat on almost all the relevant agencies, such as the English Tourist Board and the British Association of Leisure Parks, Piers and Attractions, and was awarded an OBE for this work.His daughter Amanda Thompson showcased the park by expanding her theatrical company, 'Stageworks Worldwide Productions' to be situated primarily at the Pleasure Beach. Stageworks created almost all of the shows which would become a famous trademark within Pleasure Beach, including the world-famous Hot Ice dancing extravaganza which shows as a matinee and evening performance in the Pleasure Beach arena.

Geoffrey Thompson died on 12 June 2004 immediately passing the role of Managing Director to Amanda Thompson. Nicholas Thompson became the Deputy Managing Director and Fiona Thompson became a fundamental architect (she has been praised over her work on both the Pepsi Max Big One's station and the Infusion station.) Nine days later, on 23 June, Mrs L.D Thompson, OBE died leaving the entire business to Amanda Thompson (who is the current managing director) and Nicholas Thompson who remains as the deputy managing director.

Amanda Thompson has overseen the transformation of the park to a modern, aesthetically pleasing amusement park. However, her reign has seen the removal of some rides including the Whip, Log Flume, Space Invader 2, Turtle Chase, Black Hole and Superbowl. In 2007, she introduced Infusion (relocated from the now defunct Pleasureland

Southport) and in 2009 transformed the north end of the park by introducing a new area, Bean Street FY4, which houses numerous catering outlets and bars and the Spectacular Dancing Water Show which was an eighty thousand pound investment. In 2010 she further developed the north end of the park by re-designing the area which formerly housed the old dodgems ride. The site is now a garden area with numerous water features and fanciful sculptures. The same year, Amanda brought a new dodgems ride to the park (which is now situated under the Revolution attraction.) In 2011, Nickelodeon Land will debut replacing the entire Beaver Creek area of the park. Amanda has focused on the historically important aspects of the park, the overall look of the park, the park branding; taking the park from Blackpool Pleasure Beach to Pleasure Beach Blackpool and it's current marketing name, Pleasure Beach Resort. Amanda has attempted to monetonise the park all year round by introducing ice skating at the Arena, she also introduced Adventure Golf in 2008, all of which are available to the public when the initial park is closed.

Pleasure Beach is situated along the South Shore area of Blackpool along the Fylde coast, adjacent to the promenade, opposite South Pier along Ocean Boulevard and directly above Watson road. The main entrance is to the front of the initial park and approximately 38 metres from the Pleasure Beach Casino. The ticket sales is opposite the entrance (below the Noah's Ark attraction) and is adjacent to the Globe Theatre. The main car park is to the left side of the White Tower restaurant, behind Valhalla and to the right of the Grand National station. The additional coach park is to the back of the park adjacent to the trim break section of the Pepsi Max Big One and in front of Rollercoaster. Numerous self catering kiosks are situated near to the entrance of the park. The entrance plaza is directly behind the Casino building and is themed to correspond with the Noah's Ark ride which site on top of the structure. The park is lined with tall metal gates that connect to the entrance building and the main gift shop, underneath the Noah's Ark ride. The staff entrance is towards the back of the park, behind the Grand National. Blackpool Pleasure Beach railway station is nearby.

The park is currently home to nearly 40 rides and attractions, including twelve roller coasters, of which five are wooden - the Grand National, Big Dipper, Rollercoaster, Wild Mouse and Zipper Dipper. The newest roller coaster, 'Infusion' was opened in 2007 (having been re-located from defunct sister-park, Pleasureland Southport, where it was known as TraumaTizer). When it opened in 1994, Pepsi Max Big One was the tallest, fastest and steepest roller coaster of any park in the world. It was also substantially one of the longest, measuring 5,497 feet long. Currently, the ride holds the crown as the tallest in the UK, measuring 213 ft, (235 ft above sea level.) and features a drop of 205 ft. The Pleasure Beach is one of the few parks left in the world to operate a traditional wooden Wild Mouse coaster. The ride was built entirely in house, post-World War II and is still in complete working order. It was also the first park in Europe to introduce a full inverting steel coaster, Irn-Bru Revolution, and the first to install a Space Shot ride, Tango Ice Blast which was manufactured by S&S Sports Of Utah. The park went on to launch Valhalla, which was designed by Sarner, a UK based theme park design company. Valhalla is sponsored by the Daily Star and remains prominently the 'biggest and most spectacular dark ride in the world.' At a cost of £15 million it is also the most expensive in-house attraction in the world. Later, the Pleasure Beach opened Bling, a Zierer Star Shape spin ride of which only two are operated in the world. The latest record is taken by Infusion which is the world's first suspended looping coaster entirely over water. The park has a wide variety of modern and classic-age rides and operates a separate children-themed section called 'Beaver Creek' towards the back of the park. This section of the park includes numerous small attractions suitably aimed at younger children, including a Log Flume-type attraction a 1,099 feet long junior wooden coaster and various small carousel-type attractions. The park also has its own costumed mascots which follows on from Disney's theory of character costuming regarding entertainment for younger guests.

The park has numerous food stalls, restaurants and cafés including the 'Italian Job' Italian themed restaurant, and the UK's largest Burger King chain restaurant, with two levels. It also owns the 'White Tower Restaurant' a tall white building near the front of the park which became private at the end of 2008.

BLENHEIM PALACE

Blenheim Palace is a large and monumental country house situated in Woodstock, Oxfordshire, England. It is the only non-Episcopal country house in England to hold the title of palace. The palace, one of England's largest houses, was built between 1705 and circa 1724. UNESCO recognised the palace as a World Heritage Site in 1987.

Its construction was originally intended to be a gift to John Churchill, the 1st Duke of Marlborough from a grateful nation in return for military triumph against the French and Bavarians at the Battle of Blenheim. However, it soon became the subject of political infighting, which led to Marlborough's exile, the fall from power of his Duchess, and irreparable damage to the reputation of the architect Sir John Vanbrugh.

Designed in the rare, and short-lived, English Baroque style, architectural appreciation of the palace is as divided today as it was in the 1720s. It is unique in its combined usage as a family home, mausoleum and national monument. The palace is also notable as the birthplace and ancestral home of Prime Minister Sir Winston Churchill.

The building of the palace was a minefield of political intrigue by Sarah, Duchess of Marlborough. Following the palace's completion, it became the home of the Churchill family for the following 300 years, and various members of the family have in that period wrought various changes, in the interiors, park and gardens. At the end of the 19th century, the palace and the Churchills were saved from ruin by an American marriage. Thus, the exterior of the palace remains in good repair and exactly as completed.

The estate given by the nation to Marlborough for the new palace was the manor of Woodstock, sometimes called the Palace of Woodstock, which had been a royal demesne, in reality little more than a deer park. Legend has obscured the manor's origins. King Henry I enclosed the park to contain the deer. Henry II housed his mistress Rosamund Clifford (sometimes known as "Fair Rosamund") there in a "bower and labyrinth"; a spring where she is said to have bathed remains, named after her. It seems the unostentatious hunting lodge was rebuilt many times, and had an uneventful history until Elizabeth I, before her succession, was imprisoned there by her sister Queen Mary between 1554 and 1555. Elizabeth had been implicated in the Wyatt plot, but her imprisonment at Woodstock was short, and the manor remained in obscurity until bombarded and ruined by Oliver Cromwell's troops during the Civil War. When the park was being re-landscaped as a setting for the palace the 1st Duchess wanted the historic ruins demolished, while Vanbrugh, an early conservationist, wanted them restored and made into a landscape feature. The Duchess, as so often in her disputes with her architect, won the day and the remains of the manor were swept away.

Chatsworth House

Chatsworth House is a large country house in Chatsworth, Derbyshire, England 3½ miles northeast of Bakewell (GB Grid SK260700). It is the seat of the Duke of Devonshire, and has been home to his family, the Cavendish family, since Bess of Hardwick settled at Chatsworth in 1549.

Standing on the east bank of the River Derwent, Chatsworth looks across to the low hills that divide the Derwent and Wye valleys. The house is set in expansive parkland, and backed by wooded, rocky hills rising to heather moorland and contains a unique collection of priceless paintings, furniture, Old Master drawings, neoclassical sculptures, books and other artifacts. Chatsworth has been selected as the United Kingdom's favourite country house several times.

Chatsworth house is built on sloping ground, lower on the north and west sides than on the south and east sides and has changed greatly since it was first built. The main block was re-built by the 1st Duke between 1687 and 1707, on the site of Bess of Hardwick's original Tudor mansion. The long north wing was added by the 6th Duke in the early nineteenth century.

There are many structures other than the house on the estate, including two surviving Elizabethan buildings — the Hunting Tower and Queen Mary's Bower. Flora's Temple and the 1st Duke's Greenhouse survive from the 1690s, the Stable block and bridge were built by James Paine in the 1760s and Joseph Paxton's Conservative Wall and other glasshouses date from the 19th century. The 11th Duke and Duchess added the Display Greenhouse in 1970.

Disneyland Paris

Disneyland Paris is a holiday and recreation resort in Marne-la-Vallée, a new town in the eastern suburbs of Paris, France. The complex is located 32 km (20 mi) from the centre of Paris and lies for the most part within the commune of Chessy, Seine-et-Marne.

Disneyland Paris comprises two theme parks, a retail, dining and entertainment district, and seven Disney-owned hotels. Operating since 12 April 1992, it was the second Disney resort to open outside the United States (following Tokyo Disney Resort) and the first to be owned and operated by Disney.

Disneyland Paris is owned and operated by French company Euro Disney S.C.A., a public company of which 39.78 percent of its stock is held by The Walt Disney Company, 10 percent by the Saudi Prince Alwaleed and 50.22 percent by other shareholders. The senior leader at the resort is chairman and CEO Philippe Gas.

The complex was a subject of controversy during the periods of negotiation and construction in the late 1980s and early '90s, when a number of prominent French figures voiced their opposition and protests were held by French labour unions and others. A further setback followed the opening of the resort as park attendance, hotel occupancy and revenues fell below projections. Partly as a result of the announced introduction of E.U. currency to be named the euro, the complex was renamed from Euro Disney Resort to Disneyland Paris in 1995. In July of that year, the company saw its first quarterly profit.

A second theme park, Walt Disney Studios Park, opened to the public 16 March 2002.

With 15,405,000 combined visitors to the resort's Disneyland Park and Walt Disney Studios Park in the fiscal year of 2009, it is France's and Europe's most visited Tourist site.

Following the success of Disneyland in Anaheim, California and the Walt Disney World Resort in Florida, plans to build a similar theme park in Europe emerged in 1972. Upon the leadership of E. Cardon Walker, Tokyo Disneyland opened in 1983 in Japan with instant success, forming a catalyst for international expansion. In late 1984 the heads of Disney's theme park division, Dick Nunis and Jim Cora, presented a list of approximately 1,200 possible European locations for the park.

By March 1985, the number of possible locations for the park had been reduced to four; two in France and two in Spain. Both of these nations saw the potential economic advantages of a Disney theme park and competed by offering financing deals to Disney.

Both Spanish sites were located near the Mediterranean Sea and offered a subtropical climate similar to Disney's parks in California and Florida. Disney had also shown interest in a site near Toulon in southern France, not far from Marseille. The pleasing landscape of that region, as well as its climate, made the location a top competitor for what would be called Euro Disneyland. However, thick layers of bedrock were discovered beneath the site, which would render construction too difficult. Finally, a site in the rural town of Marne-la-Vallée was chosen because of its proximity to Paris and its central location in Western Europe. This location was estimated to be no more than a four-hour drive for 68 million people and no more than a two-hour flight for a further 300 million.

Michael Eisner, Disney's CEO at the time, signed the first letter of agreement with the French government for the 20-square-kilometre (4,940-acre) site in December 1985, and the first financial contracts were drawn up during the following spring. Construction began in August 1988, and in December 1990, an information centre named "Espace Euro Disney" was opened to show the public what was being constructed. Plans for a theme park next to Euro Disneyland based on the entertainment industry, Disney-MGM Studios Europe, quickly went into development, scheduled to open in 1996 with a construction budget of US$2.3 billion. The construction manager was Bovis.

Leeds Castle and Longleat

Leeds Castle, 4 miles (6.5 km) southeast of Maidstone, Kent, England, dates back to 1119, though a manor house stood on the same site from the 9th century. The castle and grounds lie to the east of the village of Leeds, Kent, which should not be confused with the far bigger and better-known city of Leeds in West Yorkshire.

Built in 1119 by Robert de Crevecoeur to replace the earlier Saxon manor of Esledes, the castle became a royal palace in 1278 for King Edward I of England and his queen, Eleanor of Castile. Major improvements were made during his time, including the barbican, made up of three parts, each with its own entrance, drawbridge, gateway and portcullis.

Richard II's first wife, Anne of Bohemia, spent the winter of 1381 at the castle on her way to be married to the king. In 1395, King Richard II received the French chronicler Jean Froissart there, as Froissart described in his Chronicles.

Henry VIII transformed the castle for his first wife, Catherine of Aragon, and a painting commemorating his meeting with Francis I of France still hangs there. His daughter, Queen Elizabeth I was imprisoned in the castle for a time before her coronation.

Thomas Fairfax, 6th Lord Fairfax of Cameron was born at Leeds Castle. Consequently, there is a sundial at Fairfax, Virginia, telling the time in Leeds Castle, and a sundial at Leeds Castle telling the time in Virginia.

The castle escaped destruction during the English Civil War because its owners, the Culpeper family, sided with the Parliamentarians. The last private owner of the castle was the Hon. Olive, Lady Baillie, a daughter of Almeric Paget, 1st Baron Queenborough, and his first wife, Pauline Payne Whitney, an American heiress. Lady Baillie bought the castle in 1926. She redecorated the interior, first working with the French architect and designer Armand-Albert Rateau (who also oversaw exterior alterations as well as adding interior features such as a 16th century-style carved-oak staircase) and then, later, with the Paris decorator Stéphane Boudin. During WWII Lady Baillie hosted burned Commonwealth airmen at the castle as part of their recovery. Survivors remember the experience with fondness to this day. Upon her death in 1974, Lady Baillie left the castle to the Leeds Castle Foundation, a private charitable trust whose aim is to preserve the castle and grounds for the benefit of the public. The castle was opened to the public in 1976.

On 17 July 1978, the castle was the site of a meeting between the Egyptian President Anwar Sadat and Israeli Foreign Minister Moshe Dayan in preparation for the Camp David Accords.

This castle and its grounds are now a leisure destination in the county of Kent. The castle grounds have an aviary, a maze, a grotto, a golf course and what may be the world's only museum of dog collars. The castle is available to host conferences. Also seasonal hot air balloon flights are available at Leeds Castle.

Maze

The maze was constructed in 1988, using 2,400 yew trees. To the disappointment of some who use the technique of solving a maze by keeping one hand on a wall while walking through as a wall follower, the method fails at the Leeds Castle Maze, because not all 'walls' are connected.

Longleat

Longleat is an English country house, currently the seat of the Marquesses of Bath, adjacent to the village of Horningsham and near the towns of Warminster in Wiltshire and Frome in Somerset. It is noted for its Elizabethan country house, maze, landscaped parkland and safari park. The house is set in over 900 acres (364 ha) of parkland, landscaped by Capability Brown, with 8,000 acres (32.37 km2) of woods and farmland. It was the first stately home to open to the public, and also claims the first safari park outside Africa.

The house was built by Sir John Thynne, and designed mainly by Robert Smythson, after the original priory was destroyed by fire in 1567. It took 12 years to complete and is widely regarded as one of the finest examples of Elizabethan architecture in Britain. Longleat is currently occupied by Alexander Thynn, 7th Marquess of Bath, a direct descendant.

A leat is an artificial waterway or channel such as that which supplies a watermill.

SAFFRON WALDEN

Saffron Walden is a medium-sized market town in the Uttlesford district of Essex, England. It is located 12 miles (19 km) north of Bishop's Stortford, 15 miles (24 km) south of Cambridge and approx 45 miles (72 km) north of London. The town retains a rural appearance and many very old buildings dating from the medieval period onwards In 2001 the parish had a population of 15,095 although this has increased marginally since then.

There has been a village on or near the site of present day Saffron Walden since before the Roman occupation of Britain when Bronze and Iron Age tribes settled in the area. After the Romans withdrew from the country, a flourishing Anglo-Saxon town was established

With the Norman invasion of 1066, a stone church was built. The castle was constructed c.1116 A Priory, later to become Walden Abbey, was also founded under the patronage of Geoffrey de Mandeville, first Earl of Essex around 1136. The abbey was separated from the town of Walden by Holywell Field, which was enclosed in the sixteenth century to form part of the park of Audley End, the house of Sir Thomas Audley, who converted the abbey cloisters to a dwelling c. 1538-44 The inner or Little Court of the seventeenth-century house corresponds to one of the cloisters.

In 1141 the area's market was transferred to the town from nearby Newport, further increasing the area's influence The town's first charter was granted in 1300 This early town was known as Chipping Walden. The town was at first largely confined to the castle's outer bailey, but in the 13th century the Battle or Repel Ditches were built or extended, to enclose a new larger area to the south. The focus of the town moved southwards to Market Square.

In the medieval period the primary trade in Saffron Walden was in wool However, in the 16th century and 17th century the saffron crocus (crocus sativus) became widely grown in the area. The flower was precious, as extract from the stigmas, the saffron, was used in medicines, as a condiment, as a perfume, as an aphrodisiac, and as an expensive yellow dye. This industry gave its name to the town and Chipping Walden became Saffron Walden.

The town and the surrounding area, like much of East Anglia, was strongly Puritan during the 17th century. This area in particular was one heavily influenced by the Rev. John Eliot. By 1640, the Samuel Bass family and a number of others had departed for the Massachusetts Bay Colony as part of the wave of emigration that occurred during the Great Migration.

Given its theological leanings and geography, seventeenth century Saffron Walden found itself at the center of the Eastern Association during the decade of the English Civil War. In the Spring of 1647, while serving as a New Model Army headquarters, the town was visited by then Lieutenant-General of Horse, Oliver Cromwell. The parliamentarian forces were internally divided at that time and Cromwell asked to see if compromise could be found that would reunify them in purpose and perhaps avoid another flare-up of civil war.

By the end of the 18th century the saffron flower was no longer in such demand, and the flower was replaced by malt and barley. In the 1830s there were more than 30 maltings and breweries running. Although this trade was not so rewarding as the saffron, the town continued to grow throughout the 19th century, having a cattle market and building a library and other civic buildings. During this time Quakers became very active in Saffron Walden, the most influential family being the Gibsons, who aided in the construction of several buildings that remain today, such as the museum and the Town Hall.

The 1900s saw expansion of the Saffron Walden branch railway line that extended from Audley End, on the mainline from London to Cambridge, to Bartlow. This closed with the Beeching cuts in the 1960s. Some light industrial areas to the east, in particular Acrow Ltd, makes of falsework and the south of the town were added to diversify the employment. In the 1980s major expansion of housing estates to the south expanded the housing stock significantly.

Today, Saffron Walden is a flourishing and historic town. Because it has never been sacked or destroyed by fire, many of the buildings, streets and features, especially in the centre of town, date back centuries. Although the 1900s brought many changes and expansion, the character of the town and the valley in which it sits remains strongly intact.

Saffron Walden is home to the largest parish church in Essex. St. Mary the Virgin dates mainly from the end of the 15th century, when the previously existing and smaller church was extensively rebuilt in flint. In 1769 it was damaged by lightning and the repairs, carried out in the 1790s, removed many of the medieval features. The present spire was added in 1832 to replace an older 'lantern' tower. The church is 183 feet (56 m) long and the spire 193 feet (59 m) high, and is the tallest in Essex.

Saffron Walden also features the ruins of the 12th-century Walden Castle, built or expanded by Geoffrey de Mandeville, the first Earl of Essex. After the medieval period, the castle fell slowly into disuse and much of the flint was taken and used in the construction of local houses and the wall surrounding the Audley End estate. All that remains today is the ruined basement.

Nearby to the castle is the Maze, a series of circular excavations cut into the turf of the common. It is the largest turf maze in England, the main part being about 100 feet (30 m) in diameter. The earliest record of it was in 1699, and it has been extensively restored several times, most recently in 1979.

There is also a hedge maze in nearby Bridge End Gardens. The garden, which lies off Castle Street and Bridge Street, dates from the 1840s and was originally laid out by Francis Gibson, a member of the locally well-known Gibson family who were eminent Quakers, bankers and brewers. Close to the Bridge End Gardens is the Fry Art Gallery which exhibits the work of artists who had an association with Saffron Walden and north west Essex. One artist of note included in the Fry Art Gallery collection is Edward Bawden who lived in the town during the 1970s and 1980s.

Nearby is the Anglo American playing fields and monument to commemorate the American airmen and people of Saffron Walden borough that died in the Second World War.

Another tourist attraction is Audley End, a manor house built by the Earl of Suffolk in the seventeenth century on the site of the medieval Walden Abbey, which had been rebuilt by Sir Thomas Audley. When first constructed, the house was one of the largest in England. However, two thirds of it was later demolished when it was found to be difficult to maintain. The house and gardens are now owned by English Heritage and are open to the public. During the summer months concerts in the style of the BBC Proms are held here, typically an evening of music of diversity ranging from classical to rock to jazz followed by a fireworks display. Another annual fireworks display is held on the Saturday nearest to the 5 November. This event is organised by the Round Table and is held on the common - near the maze.

Nearby Audley End is the Audley End Miniature Railway, which is a 10+1?4 in (260 mm) gauge railway ride through woodland. The ride is 1.5 miles (2.4 km) long and has been part of the Saffron Walden landscape since it was opened in 1964. It is a popular site with children.

The oldest inhabited building in Saffron Walden, a 600-year-old former maltings, is now a 40-bed Youth Hostel Association youth hostel.

Saffron Walden is home to one of the finest quality concrete skate parks in Europe, One Minet Park, built by US company Dreamland.

Other sites include the Corn Exchange (now a library) and the market square around which a number of buildings of historical interest and the Town Hall are centred. Market Days are Tuesdays and Saturdays.

Schönbrunn Palace

Schönbrunn Palace is a former imperial summer residence in Vienna, Austria. One of the most important cultural monuments in the country, since the 1960s it has been one of the major tourist attractions in Vienna. The palace and gardens illustrate the tastes, interests, and aspirations of successive Habsburg monarchs.

In the year 1569, Holy Roman Emperor Maximilian II purchased a large floodplain of the Wien river beneath a hill, situated between Meidling and Hietzing, where a former owner, in 1548, had erected a mansion called Katterburg. The emperor ordered the area to be fenced and put game there such as pheasants, ducks, deer and boar, in order to serve as the court's recreational hunting ground. In a small separate part of the area, "exotic" birds like turkeys and peafowl were kept. Fishponds were built, too.

The name Schönbrunn (meaning "beautiful spring"), has its roots in an artesian well from which water was consumed by the court.

During the next century, the area was used as a hunting and recreation ground. Especially Eleonore Gonzaga, who loved hunting, spent much time there and was bequeathed the area as her widow's residence after the death of her husband, Ferdinand II. From 1638 to 1643, she added a palace to the Katterburg mansion, while in 1642 came the first mention of the name "Schönbrunn" on an invoice. The origins of the Schönbrunn orangery seem to go back to Eleonore Gonzaga as well.

The sculpted garden space between the palace and the Neptune Fountain is called the Great Parterre. The French garden, a big part of the area, was planned by Jean Trehet in 1695. It contains, among other things, a maze.

The complex however includes many more attractions: Besides the Tiergarten, the world's oldest existing zoo (founded in 1752), an orangerie erected around 1755, staple luxuries of European palaces of its type, a Palm house (replacing, by 1882, around ten earlier and smaller glass houses in the western part of the park) is noteworthy. Western parts were turned into English garden style in 1828–1852. At the outmost western edge, a botanical garden going back to an earlier arboretum was re-arranged in 1828, when the Old Palm House was built. This one is currently being restored and partly will be house a modern enclosure for Orangutans, besides a restaurant and office rooms. It will be re-opened in 2009. Lining the Great Parterre are 32 sculptures, which represent deities and virtues.

Tatton Park

Tatton Park is a historic estate in Cheshire, England, to the north of the town of Knutsford. It contains a mansion, Tatton Hall, a manor house dating from medieval times, Tatton Old Hall, gardens, a farm and a deer park of 1,000 acres (4.0 km2). It is a popular visitor attraction and hosts over 100 events annually. The estate is owned by the National Trust and administered in conjunction with Cheshire East Council.

There is evidence of human habitation in the area of the estate going back to the Iron Age. In medieval times the village of Tatton was on the site. This has since disappeared but the area of the village and its roadways are a Scheduled Ancient Monument . By the end of the 15th century the estate was owned by the Stanley family who built and occupied the Old Hall. By the 1580s this building had been enlarged and it was owned by the Brereton family. In 1598 the estate was bought by Sir Thomas Egerton, Lord Chancellor of England. Sir Thomas and his children rarely visited the estate and it was loaned to tenants. At the end of the 17th century the estate was owned by John Egerton, Sir Thomas' grandson, and he built a new house on the site of the present mansion, some 0.75 miles (1 km) to the west of the Old Hall. This mansion, Tatton Hall, was extensively altered and extended between 1780 and 1813. In 1795 the estate covered 251,000 acres (1,020 km2). The estate remained in the ownership of the Egerton family until Maurice Egerton died in 1958, leaving it to the National Trust. By that time the size of the estate had reduced to 2,000 acres (8.1 km2). The estate and its contents have been developed into a visitor attraction.

Villa Vizcaya

Vizcaya, now called the Vizcaya Museum and Gardens, is the landmark Villa and Estate of businessman James Deering, of the Deering McCormick-International Harvester fortune, on Biscayne Bay in the present day Coconut Grove district of Miami, Florida. The early 20th century Vizcaya estate also includes: the extensive Italian Renaissance gardens; the native woodland landscape; and the historic village outbuildings compound. The landscape and architecture were influenced by Veneto and Tuscan Italian Renaissance models and designed in the Mediterranean Revival architecture style. Paul Chalfin was the design director and driving force for the winter residence's resulting excellence. Miami-Dade County now owns the Vizcaya property, as the Vizcaya Museum and Gardens, which is open to the public. 'Villa Vizcaya' is served by the Vizcaya Station of the Miami Metrorail.

CHAPTER–6

ECONOMIC IMPACT OF HORTICULTURAL TOURISM

Gardens: Crompton (1993) suggested it was public parks and recreation facilities that attracted tourists to an area. Gardens vary in their type in different areas and are attractions in their own right.

Botanic Gardens: Concentrate on high quality displays including colour and form, geographical collections, plant trials, specialist collections and many more. A great deal of work is put into interpretation work such as signs and various educational programmes.

These are a major drawcard for both domestic and international visitors.

In the results of a survey in Christchurch Botanic Gardens (Jolliffe, 1976) where a question asked "What is the main reason you came to the Botanic Gardens". The most responses were, "to feed the ducks". Maybe there is a lesson there . The need for some excitement, movement or something people can relate to.

Public Gardens and Domains: these are generally nice places to go and have a high profile in the local community.

Horticultural Features: there are many of these in every town or city. Outside the town hall and in prominent places.

All to beautify the area and make it more attractive to both locals and visitors.

The survey in 1976 examined what people did in the Christchurch Botanic Gardens.

Activities in Order of Importance

1. Strolling
2. Looking at trees and plants
3. Looking at wildlife
4. Relaxing
5. Visiting conservatories

(Jolliffe 1976)

This provides a guide to the type of design elements that need to be included.

Private Gardens: contrary to popular opinion some of the best plant collections in New Zealand are in private gardens. These are owned and maintained by serious amateurs or semi-professionals.

Today many of these are open to the public either regularly, occasionally or seasonally. There may be a charge for charity or a charge to pay for the upkeep or even run as a business. Some of the better ones have associated food and beverage outlets, souvenirs, merchandise, plants ete to increase revenue.

Farms: one of the fastest growing tourism ventures in New Zealand today is Farm Stay/Home Stay. Everything from the Hobby Farm to the High Country Station is offering a range of truly NZ "get to know you" opportunities.

Associated with many of these areas are some of the country's best private gardens. In fact, in some cases the garden is the prime attraction.

Not only is it the garden but also the farm with its high number of trees planted on the land. Some of the country's largestcollection of trees either generally or in specific generic collections are to be found on farms (MacKay, 1993).

Attractions: Kiwifruit Country, Disneyland, Sea World, Dreamworld all use horticulture to enhance the quality of the visit.

Take for example Disneyland. It always looks great, is extremely well landscaped, with not a plant out of place. It is the gardens — its horticultural expertise in planning, design, planting and maintenance that sets it apart from others.

Kiwifruit Country serves to enthuse people to learn more about horticulture. Living education — and it is only a small part of the horticulture that fascinates people.

Nurseries Retail: there are the old fashioned plantsman nurseries which are a joy for the specialist to visit. However, Palmers have changed the face of nursery retailing turning it into an adventure and a day out. With its special guests Maggie Barry and Bill Ward — coffee shop, range of other garden related products and of course plants. Swafield (1992) stated "Garden centres rival shopping centres as a weekend leisure focus".

Gardens

There is a growing interest in visiting gardens. Everywhere there are garden visits organised. In the Wellington Region in August 1995, 5 or more separate organisations ran garden visits with some 150 private gardens open to the public. In addition New Zealand Rail organised a train trip to the Wairarapa to visit gardens. Palmers Garden Centre and Williams Garden Centre also organised them. The list goes on.

Deloitte Touche Tobmatsu (1993) conduct an annual visitor survey of attractions in New Zealand.

The following chart shows the dates when public and private gardens in the survey were first opened to the public:

Pre 1930	2.7%
1930-49	35.1%

1950-69	18.9%
1970-79	8.1%
1980-85	10.8%
1986-90	0%
1991-92	24.3%

Opening Hours

Gardens have the longest opening hours of all attractions. 51% of all gardens have an entrance fee.

Marketing

92% spend less than $5,000 on marketing.

Gardens have the lowest marketing budget of all attractions.

Gardens know less about visitor make up than other attractions.

When looking at this information one gets the impression that everyone is getting on the bandwagon — especially private gardens. One thing this survey does not state is the quality of those gardens, best season, outstanding feature or landscape design. This issue needs to be addressed.

Note that the majority of the visitors are not international but domestic. Of the domestic visitors I suggest a high % are local ratepayers. If the locals take their out of town visitors to the gardens are they going to feel proud of the gardens? That is the test!

Local authorities which want to attract tourists and use their parks and gardens to add to the overall landscape of the city or be an attraction have to meet the competition head on. Take a look at their parks and gardens, change them, improve them or lose the tourism race.

VISITOR NUMBERS TO GARDENS

Total visitors (includes domestic and international tourists)

Gardens 2.76 million visitors

This compares with:

Museums 3.82 million visitors

Attractions 4.09 million visitors (includes theme parks etc.)

Average number of visitors per garden 95,366

77% of all gardens have less than 30,000 visitors.

International Visitors

Estimated only 9% (248,000) of international visitors visit gardens70.3% of gardens predict an increase in visitor numbers of between 1-20%

Media Survey

In order to test the popularity of horticulture as a tourism attraction 1 looked at different media and the programmes being offered.

Television

Documentaries	Several have featured gardens. The Ellerslie Flower Show is being filmed as a documentary.
News	Various news items feature high profile horticultural events.
Palmers Garden Show	Includes gardening, garden visits, landscaping, nurseries, etc. Its ratings are extremely high.
Living Earth	Conservation, gardening, gardening visits etc.
Advertisements	Flowers, plants, gardens all feature.
Travel Programmes	Places to visit
Videos	Gardening, Gardens etc

Magazines

The following information was taken from the New Zealand Gardener August 1994, Circulation 60,000.

Advertisements	National Trust GardensSmall Acorns 15 gardens to visit Taranaki Garden FestivalEden GardenHuntly School Garden FestivalStallard Farm
Gardens to Visit	Brown Sugar Café Pams Lavender Patch
Flower shows	Ellerslie Roseworld (Christchurch) Waikato Flower Show Dunedin Rhododendron Festival Matamata Festival of Flowers Manawatu Rose & Garden
Nurseries	Cannock WoodBay bloomCross HillsCoehaven
Travel	To New CaledoniaThomas Cook Coromandel Peninsula Small Acorns 8 garden tours advertised Nelson Town and Country Tours Travel Works 4 tours overseas Travelwise 6 New Zealand and overseas toursYoungs Garden Tours East Coast
Education	Garden Marlborough Garden Galaxy — Masterton
Articles	Gardener holiday in New Caledonia

This shows the range of advertising using horticulture to promote tourism.

New Zealand Gardener 1993-94

From the index — feature articles on gardens and tourism

13	Country Gardens
13	Gardens to Visit
1	Article about gardens to visit
8	Articles on nurseries.
Radio	Gardening shows
Newspapers	Garden Sections
	Articles
	Advertising
Brochures	General

When looking at brochures promoting cities and regions parks and reserves feature strongly.

NZTB uses amazing photographs of flora, scenery, parks and gardens. The range of photographs is wide.

Brochures	Specific

Brochures of specific attractions always features plants, garden setting, views or scenery.

SPECIAL EVENTS — HORTICULTURE

Horticultural events are proving more and more popular all the time and create a major inflow of domestic tourists. The day-tripper is just as important as the overnighter.

At some point in time these events will reach market saturation reducing the likelihood of them being repeated in the future due to insufficient visitors to make it profitable.

The decline in attendance may also be caused by too many poor quality events rather than too many good events.

Other Horticulture

Looking at the nature of tourism a range of other horticultural sectors influences tourism.

Horticulture	Use
Pot plants	decoration
Cut flowers	decoration, gifts
Food	vegetables
Salads	food
Fruit	fresh fruit
Timber	souvenirs, packaging
Highway landscape	scenery
Open space	green image
Decorations	Events
Turf	Stadiums, sports grounds

The influence of horticulture is immense.

Impacts on Tourism

There are 4 major impacts of tourism. Each has its good points and bad points. Right now everyone is promoting the good points and in some cases ignoring the bad.

Economic Impact

Local authorities and other groups see tourism as a saviour creating employment and wealth in a region. Jobs are created in three ways directly, indirectly and induced. The indirect and induced jobs are as a result of the multiplier effect of tourism dollars spent in your community. There may also be jobs created in horticulture.

Environmental Impact

Natural areas often don't have a high level of development and may deteriorate rapidly and unseen to the eye. Photographs on a 12 monthly basis help if a comparison needs to be made. Use and effects on the environment must be considered under the Resource Management Act. The normal aspects of new developments are dealt with but managers must now consider the physical carrying capacity of the area.

Gardens with good paths that don't wear out, grass well maintained, vandalism minimised and with litter cleared up have a high carrying capacity. Garden areas are very suitable to develop to take pressure off natural areas.

Social carrying capacity is also important. Visitors do not mind sharing the discovery of a fine garden with 50 others. This issue is greater in National Parks where low social carrying capacity has to be managed to ensure a high quality experience.

Cultural Impact

What impact does tourism have on the New Zealand culture? What is the typical New Zealand garden? Does the number and type of visitors influence garden design? A range of issues need to be addressed.

Social Impact

How does tourism impact on the local population? Studies have shown that the constant flow of visitors can have either a negative or positive impact on the social structure of our society. Attitudes and habits will change as people interact with tourists from other cultures.

INTERRELATIONSHIPS OF IMPACTS

These impacts while dealt with separately need to be considered in an interrelated way. Managers need to understand the nature of tourism, tourist behaviour and land management issues to derive the greatest benefit from increased visitor numbers.

Case Study

The Impact of Horticulture on the Canadian Economy

Take a second and consider the following...what would be the first thing that comes to mind if you were asked to describe the Canadian horticulture industry? For many consumers I would venture to guess the first, and probably second and third, descriptor would revolve around a type/variety of fruit produced in Canada (e.g. a type of fruit, vegetable, ornamental, etc.). At what point would the industries impact on the Canadian economy be mentioned. Most likely the likes of job creation, import/exports, and role in tourism would rank way down the list. However, the economic impact of the horticulture industry on the Canadian economy is quite significant and transcends any one crop.

So let's take a quick look at two such issues, value of the industry and its role in tourism. So, how valuable is the horticulture industry to Canada? Total farm cash receipts for the horticulture industry in 2008 were estimated to be $5.8 billion or 14% of agricultural farm cash receipts (Agriculture and Agri-Food Canada - Horticulture Section). However, this value only represents cash receipts, it does not take into account any other output generated. When we account for other effects such as labour income, direct and indirect outputs resulting from the industry, the economic benefit is considerably higher. For instance, in 2004, for every $1 of output from the Ontario greenhouse industry alone, there was a $2.81 impact on the economy as a whole (Greenhouse Canada). As noted by the Niagara Regional Agricultural Economic Impact Study, horticulture sub-sectors created some of the highest economic multipliers of the industries surveyed (The Regional Municipality of Niagara), implying that the horticulture industry is having a profound impact on the Canadian economy.

Another issue that is generally not considered is the effect of horticulture on the tourism industry. Does horticulture impact the decision making process of someone thinking of traveling to Canada? According to a 2001 report by the Tourism Investment Development Office the answer is yes. The report found that garden attractions impacted the decision to travel to Ontario "a lot." Would these visitors have come without the presence of horticulture, maybe? But the presence of horticulture does have some influence on choice of destination. Whether it is production or beautification, horticulture can play a role.

In summary, the horticulture industry has a far greater impact than many people think. From impacting the economy directly, providing jobs for businesses that cater to the industry, to tourism, the horticulture industry is intrinsic to the fabric of the Canada.

CHAPTER–7

ENVIRONMENTAL IMPACTS OF HORTICULTURAL TOURISM

The quality of the environment, both natural and man-made, is essential to tourism. However, tourism's relationship with the environment is complex. It involves many activities that can have adverse environmental effects. Many of these impacts are linked with the construction of general infrastructure such as roads and airports, and of tourism facilities, including resorts, hotels, restaurants, shops, golf courses and marinas. The negative impacts of tourism development can gradually destroy the environmental resources on which it depends.

On the other hand, tourism has the potential to create beneficial effects on the environment by contributing to environmental protection and conservation. It is a way to raise awareness of environmental values and it can serve as a tool to finance protection of natural areas and increase their economic importance.

LOSS OF BIOLOGICAL DIVERSITY

Biological diversity is the term given to the variety of life on Earth and the natural patterns it forms.

The effects of loss of biodiversity:

- It threatens our food supplies, opportunities for recreation and tourism, and sources of wood, medicines and energy.
- It interferes with essential ecological functions such as species balance, soil formation, and greenhouse gas absorption.
- It reduces the productivity of ecosystems, thereby shrinking nature's basket of goods and services, from which we constantly draw.
- It destabilizes ecosystems and weakens their ability to deal with natural disasters such as floods, droughts, and hurricanes, and with human-caused stresses, such as pollution and climate change.

Tourism, especially nature tourism, is closely linked to biodiversity and the attractions created by a rich and varied environment. It can also cause loss of biodiversity when land and resources are strained by excessive use, and when impacts on vegetation, wildlife, mountain, marine and coastal environments and water resources exceed the carrying capacity. This loss of biodiversity in fact means loss of tourism potential.

INTRODUCTION OF EXOTIC SPECIES

Tourists and suppliers - often unwittingly - can bring in species (insects, wild and cultivated plants and diseases) that are not native to the local environment and that can cause enormous disruption and even destruction of ecosystems.

Depletion of the Ozone Layer

The ozone layer, which is situated in the upper atmosphere (or stratosphere) at an altitude of 12-50 kilometers, protects life on earth by absorbing the harmful wavelengths of the sun's ultraviolet (UV) radiation, which in high doses is dangerous to humans and animals. For instance, one of the reasons scientists have put forward for the global decrease of amphibian populations is increased exposure to UV radiation.

Ozone depleting substances (ODSs) such as CFCs (chlorofluorocarbon) and halons have contributed to the destruction of this layer. The tourism industry may be part of the problem; direct impacts start with the construction of new developments and continue during daily management and operations. Refrigerators, air conditioners and propellants in aerosol spray cans, amongst others, contain ODSs and are widely used in the hotel and tourism industry. Emissions from jet aircraft are also a significant source of ODSs. According to Tourism Concern, scientists predict that by 2015 half of the annual destruction of the ozone layer will be caused by air travel.

UNEP's OzonAction Programme works with governments and industries, including the tourism industry, to phase out ODSs and find safer alternatives. UNEP has developed extensive information and guidance on how many types of businesses can eliminate ODSs and contribute to preservation of the ozone layer. For further reading see the publication How the Hotel and Tourism Industry can Protect the Ozone Layer.

Climate Change

Climate scientists now generally agree that the Earth's surface temperatures have risen steadily in recent years because of an increase in the so-called greenhouse gases in the atmosphere, which trap heat from the sun. One of the most significant of these gases is carbon dioxide (CO2), which is generated when fossil fuels, such as coal, oil and natural gas are burned (e.g. in industry, electricity generation, and automobiles) and when there are changes in land use, such as deforestation. In the long run, the accumulation of CO2 and other greenhouse gases in the atmosphere can cause global climate change - a process that may already be occurring.

Global tourism is closely linked to climate change. Tourism involves the movement of people from their homes to other destinations and accounts for about 50% of traffic movements; rapidly expanding air traffic contributes about 2.5% of the production of CO2. Tourism is thus a significant contributor to the increasing concentrations of greenhouse gases in the atmosphere. (Source: Mountain Forum)

Air travel itself is a major contributor to the greenhouse effect. Passenger jets are the fastest growing source of greenhouse gas emissions. The number of international travelers is expected to increase from 594 million in 1996 to 1.6 billion by 2020, adding greatly to the problem unless steps are taken to reduce emissions. (Source: WWF)

For more information on the relationship between energy and the environment, see UNEP's Energy Programme, which provides information and publications on energy efficiency and alternative energy sources to reduce the environmental impacts of energy use and of transportation.

HOW GLOBAL ENVIRONMENTAL IMPACTS AFFECT TOURISM

Natural Disasters

Catastrophes like floods, earthquakes, wildfires, volcanoes, avalanches, drought and diseases can have a serious effect on inbound and domestic tourism and thus on local tourism industries. The outbreak of the foot and mouth disease epidemic in England earlier this year (2001), for instance, has severely affected Great Britain's inbound tourism market. A BHA/Barclays Hospitality Business Trends Survey found that 75% of hotels in England, 81% in Scotland and 85% in Wales continued to be affected by the foot and mouth outbreak, and over 60% forecast a decline in business in the June-September 2001 period.

Climate Change

Tourism not only contributes to climate change, but is affected by it as well. Climate change is likely to increase the severity and frequency of storms and severe weather events, which can have disastrous effects on tourism in the affected regions. Some of the other impacts that the world risks as a result of global warming are drought, diseases and heat waves.

These negative impacts can keep tourists away from the holiday destinations. Global warming may cause:

- Less snowfall at ski resorts, meaning a shorter skiing seasons in the Alpine region. In already hot areas like Asia and the Mediterranean, tourists will stay away because of immense heat, and out of fear of diseases and water shortages.
- Harm to vulnerable ecosystems such as rainforests and coral reefs because of rising temperatures and less rainfall. A major risk to coral reefs is bleaching, which occurs when coral is stressed by temperature increases, high or low levels of salinity, lower water quality, and an increase in suspended sediments. These conditions cause the zooxanthallae (the single-celled algae which forms the colors within the coral) to leave the coral. Without the algae, the coral appears white, or "bleached" - and rapidly dies. The Great Barrier Reef, which supports a US$ 640 million tourism industry, has been experiencing coral bleaching events for the last 20 years. (Source: EXN)
- Rising sea levels, the result of melting glaciers and polar ice. Higher sea levels will threaten coastal and marine areas with widespread floods in low-lying countries and island states, increasing the loss of coastal land. Beaches and islands that are major tourism attractions may be the first areas to be affected.

- Increased events of extreme weather, such as tornadoes, hurricanes and typhoons. These are already becoming more prevalent in tourist areas in the Caribbean and South East Asia. Hurricane Mitch in 1998, for instance, heavily affected tourism in the Caribbean. Wind damage, storm waves, heavy rains and flooding caused major losses in the local tourism sector.

DEPLETION OF NATURAL RESOURCES

Tourism development can put pressure on natural resources when it increases consumption in areas where resources are already scarce.

Water Resources

Water, and especially fresh water, is one of the most critical natural resources. The tourism industry generally overuses water resources for hotels, swimming pools, golf courses and personal use of water by tourists. This can result in water shortages and degradation of water supplies, as well as generating a greater volume of waste water..

In dryer regions like the Mediterranean, the issue of water scarcity is of particular concern. Because of the hot climate and the tendency of tourists to consume more water when on holiday than they do at home, the amount used can run up to 440 liters a day. This is almost double what the inhabitants of an average Spanish city use.

Golf course maintenance can also deplete fresh water resources. In recent years golf tourism has increased in popularity and the number of golf courses has grown rapidly. Golf courses require an enormous amount of water every day and, as with other causes of excessive extraction of water, this can result in water scarcity. If the water comes from wells, overpumping can cause saline intrusion into groundwater. Golf resorts are more and more often situated in or near protected areas or areas where resources are limited, exacerbating their impacts.

Local Resources

Tourism can create great pressure on local resources like energy, food, and other raw materials that may already be in short supply. Greater extraction and transport of these resources exacerbates the physical impacts associated with their exploitation. Because of the seasonal character of the industry, many destinations have ten times more inhabitants in the high season as in the low season. A high demand is placed upon these resources to meet the high expectations tourists often have (proper heating, hot water, etc.).

Land Degradation

Important land resources include minerals, fossil fuels, fertile soil, forests, wetland and wildlife. Increased construction of tourism and recreational facilities has increased the pressure on these resources and on scenic landscapes. Direct impact on natural resources, both renewable and nonrenewable, in the provision of tourist facilities can be caused by the use of land for accommodation and other infrastructure provision, and the use of building materials.

Forests often suffer negative impacts of tourism in the form of deforestation caused by fuel wood collection and land clearing. For example, one trekking tourist in Nepal - and area already suffering the effects of deforestation - can use four to five kilograms of wood a day.

POLLUTION

Tourism can cause the same forms of pollution as any other industry: air emissions, noise, solid waste and littering, releases of sewage, oil and chemicals, even architectural/ visual pollution.

Air Pollution and Noise

Transport by air, road, and rail is continuously increasing in response to the rising numbe reported that the number of international air passengers worldwide rose from 88 million in 1972 to 344 million in 1994. One consequence of this increase in air transport is that tourism now accounts for more than 60% of air travel and is therefore responsible for an important share of air emissions. One study estimated that a single transatlantic return flight emits almost half the CO2 emissions produced by all other sources (lighting, heating, car use, etc.) consumed by an average person yearly. (Mayer Hillman, Town & Country Planning magazine, September 1996. Source: MFOE).

Transport emissions and emissions from energy production and use are linked to acid rain, global warming and photochemical pollution. Air pollution from tourist transportation has impacts on the global level, especially from carbon dioxide (CO2) emissions related to transportation energy use. And it can contribute to severe local air pollution. Some of these impacts are quite specific to tourist activities. For example, especially in very hot or cold countries, tour buses often leave their motors running for hours while the tourists go out for an excursion because they want to return to a comfortably air-conditioned bus.

Noise pollution from airplanes, cars, and buses, as well as recreational vehicles such as snowmobiles and jet skis, is an ever-growing problem of modern life. In addition to causing annoyance, stress, and even hearing loss for it humans, it causes distress to wildlife, especially in sensitive areas. For instance, noise generated by snowmobiles can cause animals to alter their natural activity patterns.

Solid waste and Littering

In areas with high concentrations of tourist activities and appealing natural attractions, waste disposal is a serious problem and improper disposal can be a major despoiler of the natural environment - rivers, scenic areas, and roadsides. For example, cruise ships in the Caribbean are estimated to produce more than 70,000 tons of waste each year. Today some cruise lines are actively working to reduce waste-related impacts. Solid waste and littering can degrade the physical appearance of the water and shoreline and cause the death of marine animals.

In mountain areas, trekking tourists generate a great deal of waste. Tourists on expedition leave behind their garbage, oxygen cylinders and even camping equipment. Such practices degrade the environment with all the detritus typical of the developed world, in remote areas that have few garbage collection or disposal facilities. Some trails in the Peruvian Andes and in Nepal frequently visited by tourists have been nicknamed "Coca-Cola trail" and "Toilet paper trail".

Sewage

Construction of hotels, recreation and other facilities often leads to increased sewage pollution. Wastewater has polluted seas and lakes surrounding tourist attractions, damaging the flora and fauna. Sewage runoff causes serious damage to coral reefs because it stimulates the growth of algae, which cover the filter-feeding corals, hindering their ability to survive. Changes in salinity and siltation can have wide-ranging impacts on coastal environments. And sewage pollution can threaten the health of humans and animals.

Aesthetic Pollution

Often tourism fails to integrate its structures with the natural features and indigenous architectural of the destination. Large, dominating resorts of disparate design can look out of place in any natural environment and may clash with the indigenous structural design.

A lack of land-use planning and building regulations in many destinations has facilitated sprawling developments along coastlines, valleys and scenic routes. The sprawl includes tourism facilities themselves and supporting infrastructure such as roads, employee housing, parking, service areas, and waste disposal.

Physical Impacts

Attractive landscape sites, such as sandy beaches, lakes, riversides, and mountain tops and slopes, are often transitional zones, characterized by species-rich ecosystems. Typical physical impacts include the degradation of such ecosystems.

An ecosystem is a geographic area including all the living organisms (people, plants, animals, and microorganisms), their physical surroundings (such as soil, water, and air), and the natural cycles that sustain them. The ecosystems most threatened with degradation are ecologically fragile areas such as alpine regions, rain forests, wetlands, mangroves, coral reefs and sea grass beds. The threats to and pressures on these ecosystems are often severe because such places are very attractive to both tourists and developers.

Physical impacts are caused not only by tourism-related land clearing and construction, but by continuing tourist activities and long-term changes in local economies and ecologies.

Physical Impacts of Tourism Development

- Construction activities and infrastructure development

The development of tourism facilities such as accommodation, water supplies, restaurants and recreation facilities can involve sand mining, beach and sand dune erosion, soil erosion and extensive paving. In addition, road and airport construction can lead to land degradation and loss of wildlife habitats and deterioration of scenery.

In Yosemite National Park (US), for instance, the number of roads and facilities have been increased to keep pace with the growing visitor numbers and to supply amenities, infrastructure and parking lots for all these tourists. These actions have caused habitat loss in the park and are accompanied by various forms of pollution including air pollution from automobile emissions; the Sierra Club has reported "smog so thick that Yosemite Valley could not be seen from airplanes". This occasional smog is harmful to all species and vegetation inside the Park. (Source: Trade and Environment Database)

- Deforestation and intensified or unsustainable use of land

Construction of ski resort accommodation and facilities frequently requires clearing forested land. Coastal wetlands are often drained and filled due to lack of more suitable sites for construction of tourism facilities and infrastructure. These activities can cause severe disturbance and erosion of the local ecosystem, even destruction in the long term.

- Marina development

Development of marinas and breakwaters can cause changes in currents and coastlines. Furthermore, extraction of building materials such as sand affects coral reefs, mangroves, and hinterland forests, leading to erosion and destruction of habitats. In the Philippines and the Maldives, dynamiting and mining of coral for resort building materials has damaged fragile coral reefs and depleted the fisheries that sustain local people and attract tourists.

Overbuilding and extensive paving of shorelines can result in destruction of habitats and disruption of land-sea connections (such as sea-turtle nesting spots). Coral reefs are especially fragile marine ecosystems and are suffering worldwide from reef-based tourism developments. Evidence suggests a variety of impacts to coral result from shoreline development, increased sediments in the water, trampling by tourists and divers, ship groundings, pollution from sewage, overfishing, and fishing with poisons and explosives that destroy coral habitat.

Physical Impacts from Tourist Activities

Trampling Tourists using the same trail over and over again trample the vegetation and soil, eventually causing damage that can lead to loss of biodiversity and other impacts. Such damage can be even more extensive when visitors frequently stray off established trails.

Trampling impacts on vegetation	Trampling impacts on soil
Breakage and bruising of stems	Loss of organic matter
Reduced plant vigor	Reduction in soil macro porosity
Reduced regeneration	Decrease in air and water permeability
Loss of ground cover	Increase in run off
Change in species composition	Accelerated erosion

Source: University of Idaho

- **Anchoring and other marine activities:** In marine areas (around coastal waters, reefs, beach and shoreline, offshore waters, uplands and lagoons) many tourist activities occur in or around fragile ecosystems. Anchoring, snorkeling, sport fishing and scuba diving, yachting, and cruising are some of the activities that can cause direct degradation of marine ecosystems such as coral reefs, and subsequent impacts on coastal protection and fisheries.
- **Alteration of ecosystems by tourist activities:** Habitat can be degraded by tourism leisure activities. For example, wildlife viewing can bring about stress for the animals and alter their natural

behavior when tourists come too close. Safaris and wildlife watching activities have a degrading effect on habitat as they often are accompanied by the noise and commotion created by tourists as they chase wild animals in their trucks and aircraft. This puts high pressure on animal habits and behaviors and tends to bring about behavioral changes. In some cases, as in Kenya, it has led to animals becoming so disturbed that at times they neglect their young or fail to mate.

CHAPTER–8

CULTURAL IMPACT OF HORTICULTURAL TOURISM

The impact that tourism has on the cultural lives of communities is one of the most important issues debated by tourism researchers and academics today. There is an increasingly growing concern that tourism development is leading to destinations losing their cultural identity by catering for the perceived needs of tourists.

Although they take longer to appear, the cultural consequences of tourist activity have the potential to be much more damaging in the long term than environmental or social effects. In many countries, tourists are not sensitive to local customs, traditions and standards. Offence is given without intent, as tourists are short-stay visitors carrying with them their own cultural norms and behavioural patterns. They are usually unwilling to change these norms for a temporary stay – and may be unaware that these norms are offensive to the host community.

When we approach a natural metaphor with honest senses, we can conclude nothing teleological about it. It simply is. Nature exhibits no apparent aims to its chances and cycles except those imposed by an observer. For this reason the metaphor of a plant's growth and reproduction seems particularly apt for human culture, taking culture to mean something both personal, and interconnected among individuals.

A seed finds fertile conditions, sprouts, and grows tenuously to a seedling. The seedling weathers adversity by putting down deep roots for anchorage, sustenance and nourishment. A tall stem grows upward to the light, with wider leaves to catch the energy of the sun. The leaves and roots trade water and food. New branches and leaves unfurl, building on the structure that came up underneath them. Finally when the season is right, at the very tips and heights of the plant bright buds appear. At great expense, and with tremendous preparation, the plant sustains the buds, as the buds open into brilliant flowers of signature varieties. They cross-pollinate with other plants, and before they pass away, produce seeds of tremendous variation, some of marvelous potency. Most seeds effectively imitate the plants which have produced them, others have mutated the line through other influences, or might remarkably hold within themselves some unprecedented qualities. The seeds which fall down on unreceptive soils are left to perish. Only a few of many seeds will scatter and take root in soils conducive to their germination. From those rare beginnings however, whole new plants — cultures, in various senses — will grow. And this history will repeat, but differently.

Now what can a 'naturalist' of cultures claim was the aim of a culture? When we consider that all those many who play the parts of roots, leaves, and stems build on the patterns established by seeds, we might understandably conclude that making definitive "seeds" would constitute the purpose of a culture. Not only does a culture follow in the pattern laid down by its founders, but through its propagation in seeds, a culture often lives on in similar forms.

And, perhaps we would add the "flowers" to that purpose for being instrumental in the creation of the seeds that follow in the wake of their brilliant and colorful season.

And observing that the precedence of flowering involved a massive contribution and focus to draw up the superfluity of energies evident in the sexual outburst of the flowers, and their casual self-sacrifice, we might conclude that although the flowers of a culture lead ephemeral lives their transcendence supplies the aim of the whole effort — whether those playing the parts of striving continually in support know it or not, or perhaps grasp it in the vaguest notions of "posterity" or "my children" or "living on through my descendants."

But is it not also true that without those playing roots, stems, and leaves to the young buds, such an act — such an existence — would have been impossible? So much goes into a life of individual glory, that many lives must precede heretofore as though to prepare, with a cultivation of far too much complicated chance to trace. And then it is usually those who follow a precedent who establish the next rejuvenation, after these "seeds" lie fallow for a while, and then establish a whole new pattern of life like the old, but new, and renewed. In turn this growth will sanctify its great efforts in the service of those valuations held as important by the lineage — held aloft to the sun, as it were, on display for all to see, and for fulfillment again in the seeds of the future.

All in this cycle play instrumental roles. There can be no fertility without a plant — a decadent one sometimes, and thus desperate to survive, yet always commanding resources sufficient for 'superfluous' expenditure, and more if healthy. Similarly, there can be no plants made of *many* without fertile *ones*, potent *ones*, differentiable *ones*. Therefore it would seem natural for the many to help the remarkable with special effort; it also would seem natural for the remarkable to be especially dependent on the efforts of supporters before them to make them possible, and followers after them to realize their propagation.

Specific cultures we can certainly assess, but we can make no abstract judgment of rank among the roles adopted by each type of person, simply because we are often predisposed to notice one kind over another. And so, the observer of the thrust of cultures of every kind and size, from the group of a few to a civilization, can only step back without such judgment and marvel at the complexities of nature in its infinite recombinations and growths.

In the real world the difficulty of understanding cultural ecology is not only that **(a)** the cultures I have likened to organisms influence one another unpredictably, in cooperative, competitive and indeterminate effects, and not only that **(b)** growth and change seem invisible or difficult to observe — an acceptable history of a given idea or school of thought might involve hundreds or thousands of scrutable regenerations, and more inscrutable ones — but also that **c.** the growth of cultures large or small cannot be isolated. Rather the roles of individuals overlap extensively in complex ways, presenting a forbidding and impossibly tangled overgrowth of jungle to the social observer. In the complex ecology of cultural interdependence, one who plays the root for one context might become the seed to another, later or at the same time. We might find a flower and its seed in different stages of the same figure. The types do not sort themselves for our convenience (although nature takes care of itself, it seems). It is for this reason that most simplify the process of understanding at the cost of a tremendous biases and myopias, probably either towards the more singular figures akin to flowers and seeds, or to the collective assumptions of soils and plants as falsely-distinct wholes, masses, and historical processes, made faceless.

Thirteenth-century Richard de Fournival discusses his "garden" of manuscripts in *La biblionomia*. This catalog shows the rows of his plantings: about three hundred manuscripts entered the founding collection of the Sorbonne of which forty of Fournival's have survived. The duke of Berry, most famous for his manuscript of the calendar months, utilized the insignia of vegetative "roots" to designate his manuscripts. Piero de' Medici, father of Lorenzo the Magnificent, created a *studiolo* (a study) in the Medici Palace, Via Larga, Florence. The twelve calendar months by Luca della Robbia on the ceiling are a visual cataloging system pointing out the twelve categories of Piero's classical and Christian books below, color-coded in the written catalogs of 1456 and 1464–1465 (Horowitz, 2003).

Isabella d'Este's second suite of *schaleria, studiolo,* grotto, and garden created an atmosphere of a garden of virtues, as in the Mantegna painting *Pallas Expelling the Vices from the Garden of Virtue* (1499–1502) which hung in the *studiolo* (now in the Louvre). Hovering in a cloud on the right are the three cardinal virtues; below in the distance, a pleasant landscape seen through the tree-lined archways reveals vices fleeing and new growth growing from old roots; in the foreground on the left is the Mother of Virtue imprisoned in a tree; and in the center, vices pollute the pond. Minerva (Pallas Athene) and two goddesses enter and seek to bring about a return to a garden of virtue.

The analogy of "culture" and horti"culture" is evident in many languages. The tree catalog of the library of Saint-Lambrecht, a painted panel by Michel Boeckyn (1688–1742), utilizes the common image of a tree of knowledge, with the various branches of knowledge rising from a trunk (fig. 4, Masson, 1981). One might plant a collection of books or other valuables, many might labor in the fields of scholarship and the arts, and a society devoted to cultivating the arts might create an abundant culture. French King Francis I (r. 1515–1547) was praised by his courtiers for his cultivation of the humanist virtues, which are equally evident in his manuscript collection, in the flowery ephemeral art of his royal entries, and in the flowers and fruit ornamenting the wall paintings in the Galerie Francis I, Fontainebleau. The analogy of writing to agricultural productivity, like the analogy of collecting to hunting, also helped make these cultural activities appropriately aristocratic.

Agricultural abundance ornamenting cultural institutions was so prevalent in the eighteenth century that it barely receives comment; note especially the decoration of the rotunda library of the Radcliffe Camera, Oxford, and of the stucco ceiling at the entrance to the Ashmolean Museum, Oxford. In the mid-nineteenth century, the upper walls of the main reading room of the Bibliothèque nationale were painted with illusionistic windows revealing sky and treetops. The implication that natural vegetative growth encourages the growth of the mind was expressed in the medieval tradition of drawings of a scholar in a study with an open cupboard showing fruit.

Some Exercises in Applied Thought and Discussion

1a) Take for example Socrates as the flower, and Plato as the seed, not only in the sense of propagation, but also *mutation*. Assume for the moment the validity of the analogy (which is certainly debatable). Consider this application of the metaphor as outlined above.

1b) If we consider this metaphor further, who were the people who formed the instrumental, supportive plant compared to the famous figures of Socrates and Plato? Secondly, what generation of plant, flower, and seed came before their own plant? Thirdly, what soil and conditions proved receptive to the seed of Plato's influence?

2a) Alternately, consider Jesus of Nazareth as the flower, and Paul of Tarsus the seed, not only in the sense of propagation, but also mutation. Assume for the moment the validity of the analogy (which is certainly debatable). Consider this application of the metaphor as outlined above.

2b) Again, try to identify the plant in the metaphor — who else was instrumental, besides the famous figures of Jesus and Paul? Secondly, what generation of plant, flower, and seed came before their own plant? Thirdly, what soil and conditions proved receptive to the seed of Paul's influence?

3) Consider the possibility of Socrates and Plato as the first generation, or "first coming" of the dynamic between Jesus and Paul centuries later — or at least an earlier instance of a cycle that would repeat.

As thinking points, here are some possible parallels in relationships between a) Jesus and Paul and the precursor b) Socrates and Plato:

- Both Plato and Paul founded or spread mystical or religious cults, Platonism and Xtianity.
- The student of each pair had wider influence than the mentor.
- Paul was influenced by Plato (directly and/or unconsciously), as indicated by apparent similarities between Platonism and Xtian metaphysics.
- Distortion of teachings is a common allegation against both Plato and Paul.
- One can charge that revenge for mentor's persecution and murder was an influence on both Plato and Paul's life works, for the sake of whose philosophies said murder was interpreted as a sacrifice.

4) Would a similar kind of analysis to that applied above in 1) and 2) apply to other examples of cultural influence, writ large or small? What about Karl Marx and Vladimir Lenin, for instance? Friedrich Nietzsche and Sigmund Freud? Alfred Korzybski and Robert Anton Wilson? Gilbert Ryle and Daniel Dennett? Aristotle and Ayn Rand? Jeremy Bentham and John Stuart Mill? Laozi and Zhuangzi? As you think through any of these cases, remember not to think of them simply as a duo in isolation, but as inheritors of previous or parallel cultural generations as well.

5) Instead of Socrates and Plato, what about applying the analogy to Plato and Aristotle? Rather than Aristotle and Ayn Rand, what about Nietzsche and Ayn Rand? Or, for readers familiar with my writing, what about Nietzsche and myself? See if you find that questioning the validity of the horticultural analogy of cultural influence in a particular historical case helps to clarify the depth and nature of such connections.

6) Suppose you take one recognizable, and clearly significant figure — say Jean-Jacques Rousseau, who has been linked to socialism, environmentalism, social contract theory, and many other strains of thought in cultural dynamics — and then look for the rest of the metaphor. Do you find a place for Rousseau in the growth of a culture? If so did you classify him as a seed, flower, or otherwise? Or, did you decide that the horticultural metaphor model did not fit, and that trying to fill it in would distort the facts? What if you could put Rousseau in more than one role? (If you haven't the slightest idea of how to do any of this with Rousseau, pick some other significant figure who interests you more and try this exercise again.)

7) I have focused on major figures in the history of ideas above, but most if not all readers will probably have an easier time with specific examples of culture familiar to them personally, which may or may not involve famous names. (Even those very well educated in history will often lack too much information about others' distant lives to make educated guesses.) For example culture can include arts and media of all kinds. Culture includes basic operative ideas, sensibilities, and behaviors which might be acquired from family, friends, mentors, authorities or adversaries in the course of life. Think of what kinds of culture personally interest or otherwise affect you most, and think about their sources in terms of the fertile analogy employed previously. Who cultivated these cultures, and in what roles? Finally, what parts in the cycles of *your* cultures would you prefer to play?

CASE STUDY

Jammu & Kashmir Horticulture Tourism

The Jammu and Kashmir government has decided to strengthen agriculture, tourism, horticulture and handicrafts in the state and empower people by making them self-sufficient, chief minister Omar Abdullah has said.

"The honour and dignity of the people depends on their economic independence which can be only achieved if the population is self-reliant. The government is working tirelessly to strengthen the economy of the state," he said.

Omar was addressing the largest ever 'Kissan Mela' yesterday in Baramulla, 52km from Srinagar.

He said the state government has given special focus to agriculture, horticulture, handicrafts and tourism as they are the mainstay of Kashmir's economy.

The chief minister emphasised the need to blend modern agricultural technology with conventional methods and called for a comprehensive policy to make agriculture an economic hub, especially for the educated youth.

"The vast potential of economic activities in agriculture and allied sectors has to be scientifically harnessed and young persons persuaded to take up profitable ventures in this field," he said.

Under the Krishi Kissan Yojna, about Rs122 crore were being spent this year on the agriculture sector against Rs40 crore last year, Omar said.

Rs50 crore has been spent on popularizing new technology as against Rs17 crores last year, he added.

Omar said it was important to build buffer fertilizer stocks and underscored the significance of hybrid and improved varieties of seeds.

On the National Saffron Mission launched with the Centre's assistance, Omar said the Rs376 crore project was aimed at restoring the pristine glory of 'Kashmir Saffron' and make it a reputed brand in the international market competing with Iran and Spain.

On the production and marketing of fruit, he said it was highly encouraging that despite climatic vagaries, the state's horticulture produce this year registered remarkable increase.

The hindrance in the transportation of fruit at the inception of the marketing season due to the law and order situation was tackled by the government successfully, ensuring its smooth export, he said.

"I am personally monitoring the transshipment process, receiving daily reports about the dispatches to different terminal markets," Omar said.

The chief minister said that efforts are required to restore Kashmir silk and give new dimension to sericulture in the state.

AMERICAN CULTURE AND HORTICULTURE

Prof. Chas. Joly, in the volume of the Journal de la Societe Nation-ale d'Horticulture, pays a liberal compliment to the progress of horticulture in America. He has seen the addresses of 8,000 nursery and seedsmen of America, and regards the successful establishment of a Nurseryman's Association, such as met recently at Dayton, as a mark of horticultural progress well worthy of European admiration. He remarks on the wonderfully active and useful career of our horticultural societies, and shows particularly how much the Massachusetts Society has done for America. Vine culture in the United States is represented truly as having taken a wonderful leap in horticultural progress. He repeats what has been stated before, and seems to give credence to the report that an immense quantity of American wine is sent to France, and there re-shipped to America with French brands, so as to satisfy those who firmly believe only that which comes from abroad can be good for anything. He gives great credit to the governments of those States which encourage science, and especially to those which have appointed State entomologists, whose duty it is to "study all that concerns the parasites of the vegetable kingdom in their several latitudes." Altogether, we have seldom read a more appreciative essay on American gardening than this excellent production of Prof. Joly's pen.

World Horticultural Expo Garden

Sitting in the northeast suburbs (6 kilometers from the city center) of Kunming, the World Horticultural Expo Garden is a venue for the 1999 Kunming International Horticulture Exposition. It is a first-class Daguanyuan (Grand View Garden), which has typical Chinese and local Yunnan characteristics. The World Horticultural Expo Garden is about 218 hectares (nearly 540 acres) in area, with vegetation coverage reaching 76.7%, including gradual slopes of 120 hectares (about 300 acres). And 10% to 15% of the garden is covered by water. Gardening works of many domestic and foreign places are on display in the garden.

Kunming World Horticultural Expo Garden is now divided into five big exhibition halls, seven special gardens and three outdoor showplaces. The five exhibition halls include the China Hall, the International Hall, the Man and Nature Hall, the Science and Technology Hall and the Grand Greenhouse. Seven theme gardens are the Vegetable and Fruit Garden, the Bamboo Garden, the Bonsai Plants Garden, the Tea Garden, the Medicinal Herb Garden, the Tree Garden and the Garden of Famous Flowers and Strange Stones (This Garden was found after the 1999 Kunming International Horticulture Exposition). The three outdoor showplaces are the International Exhibition Gardens, the Domestic Exhibition Gardens and the Exhibition Area for Enterprises.

Going straight forward after entering the garden, visitors will see the Grand Greenhouse. With total area of 3,630 square meters (about 0.9 acre), it includes four exhibition areas: the Tropical Plant Exhibition Area, the Temperate Plants Exhibition Area, Plants at High and Cold Elevations Areas (3,000 meters or more above the sea level), Exhibition Centre and Photos Exhibition Area.

After visiting the Grand Greenhouse, the tourists can see the Domestic Exhibition Gardens to the north. It is composed of 34 sections according to China's provinces and regions. With different characteristics, these provincial gardens stand in four solid lines. Walking forward to the World Horticultural Expo Garden, visitors encounter the International Exhibition Gardens, which include 33 sections in total. The five big exhibition halls and the seven special gardens are scattered in the garden.

Kunming World Horticultural Expo Garden transplants and cultivates 2,551 kinds of plants with a total census of more than 2 million. Among them, 112 categories are rare and endangered species. With the theme of Man and Nature, the Garden shows that human beings are interrelated with Nature in a harmonious way.

As the only remains of International Horticulture Exposition, Kunming Expo Garden has created the best record in history. At the same time, it has set a slew of world records in Guinness, such as the largest in area, the fastest in pace of construction and the most in species of plants on display.

Sequoia National Park-Redwoods

Redwood and national parks are located in the United States of America along the coast of north California, consisting of a combined area of 131,983 acres. This park has 35 groves of giant Sequoias (*Sequoia sempervirens*). In this park, one of the largest oldest living things in the world is the General Sherman tree, which is estimated to be more than 3,500 years old, standing 272 feet high and 37 feet in diameter. Also this forest is home to many coniferous evergreen trees.

Amazon Jungle

This most endangered rain-forest covers most Amazon basin of South America. The total area covered by this jungle is 1.4 billion acres, happening a territory of nine nations Brazil, Peru, Colombia, Venezuela, Ecuador, Bolivia, Guyana, Suriname, and French Guiana. However Brazil contains the majority of the forest. It was short-listed in 2008 as a candidate to one of the "new seven wonders of nature" by the "new seven wonders of the world" foundation.

This jungle contains atleast 40,000 plant species. It has been estimated that about one square mile might contain 750 tree and 1500 plant species. Brazil grow nuts in its part of forest. The nuts are inside a round grapefruit size ball. Each ball can contain 20 to 25 nuts. About one-third of all coconuts grown can be found in is South American rainforest. Ferns of all varieties, from very small to large bushes, hibiscus, periwinkle and several varieties of orchids, palm trees, vines climbing up looking for the sun also make this their home. Among fruit products of this rainforest are pineapples, mangos and guavas.

Wisteria House

Wisteria has been determined by the Guinness Book of World Records to be the largest blossoming plant in the world. The single wisteria vine covers over an acre in size. It has more than a million blossoms and weighs 250 tons. This horticultural wonder has already engulfed one home and is on its way towards another and can be seen by taking a trip to Sierra Madre.

Xochimilco Floating Gardens in Mexico: Xochimilco means "Garden of Flowers." Raised agricultural fields called chinampas, dating back to the Aztecs, are surrounded by canals. Alternating weeds and earth are packed inside cane frames that are rooted to the lake floor by trees planted along the edges of the field. The chinampas are living examples of sustainable agriculture but a historical artifact. Today's farmers scrape the organic debris from the canals to use as fertilizer in their agricultural gardens. In the winter they plant flowers and in the summer you will see fruit, corn, and summer vegetables in the canals.

Garden of Taj Mahal: This garden is designed in Islamic style of architecture and symbolizes spirituality. Total area of Taj complex is 580m by 300m, of which Taj garden alone covers 300m by 300m. The central raised pool is divided into 16 flower beds, making a total of 64 beds in all, each bed containing 400 plants which includes flowers, birds, and fruit trees. The fruit trees and cypress are planted to maintain symmetry. This garden is a man-made garden based on the arrangements of nature.

Garden of Buckingham Palace: It is situated at rear of Buckingham palace. It covers 42 acre area and 2.5 miles of gravel paths. Plantation in this garden is varied and exotic, with a mulberry tree dating back to the times of James 1 of England. A large 19th-century lake graced by a flock of flamingos and the Waterloo Vase is one of the most notable feature of the palace. Indian chestnut, silver maple and swamp cypress are some of the elegant trees in this garden.

Yokohama Rock Gardens, Japan

These gardens have been made in the traditional Japanese way. Of which rock and water are prominent features. These gardens have their roots in the 13th century. So guys these are the seven horticultural wonders of the world. Hope you found this post very interesting as well as very informative. If you've really enjoyed it then please give me your feedback though your comments. It's almost whole day finished now working on this post, I'm really broken, so pass your comments generously to prove my effort meaningful.

CHAPTER–9

SOCIAL IMPACT OF HORTICULTURAL TOURISM

Tourism in the small islands context involves people who come from other countries for the pleasure of visiting the island environment. Since tourists spend money on travel, hotels, food, entertainment and recreation, they can be an important source of income and thus of economic development for islands with few other possible sources of revenue.

The tourists who come to the islands have been attracted by their image of the island environment: sun and sea, white sandy beaches and waving palm trees, lush vegetation and friendly natives. The reality is never quite the same as the tourist image, but while it can be different, it should not disappoint them or tourism will ultimately fail. People do not come several thousand kilometres to see the same dirt, pollution, industry and degraded environments that they have at home.

Tourism thus depends on the quality of the environment for its success, and good tourist development requires the protection and even the improvement of the environment. The most important tourism resources are the natural beauty of the island, their distinctive or exotic character, their recreation possibilities, and the cultural interest of the people. The hotels, resorts, transportation networks, recreation facilities and other tourism infrastructure can complement but never completely replace the dependence on environmental resources.

The basic problem with tourism development is that tourism facilities and the tourists themselves have impacts on the environment. If care is not taken, the tourism development itself can gradually destroy the environmental resources on which it depends. This problem can be particularly serious on tropical islands where the environment is fragile and easily degraded, and where the small scale of the island means that even moderate tourism development can have a proportionately large impact.

Once there was talk about three kinds of untruths: lies, damned lies and statistics. Today some would happily add the new catch-phrase 'sustainable development' to the trio. It is complex, it is hard to define, it is elusive-perhaps non-achievable-but nevertheless most agree it is something we must strive for. Recent history has convinced politicians, catchment managers, primary producers and the whole community of consumers that we need increased effort towards sustainability in use and management of our resources.

The rapid growth of the landcare movement is evidence that primary producers accept this need. Brian Scarsbrick, Chairman of Landcare Australia Limited, claims that some 35 per cent of rural producers are now involved Australia-wide. One of the goals of landcare, as described in Queensland's *Decade of Landcare Plan* (1991, p. vii) is to 'Maintain the economic viability of agricultural production within an ecologically sustainable framework'. Landcare bodies and catchment committees are working with industry organisations and government agencies to develop farming systems and Codes of Best Practice to achieve this objective.

Sustainability is surely a big issue in the minds of tree and nut crop growers who need to plan well ahead, and face delayed returns as well as limited flexibility once the trees are in the ground. Issues of most concern are probably the ability of land and water resources to maintain productive growth, the financial impact of doing whatever needs to be done to maintain these resources in good condition, and perhaps the possibility of depressed market returns should many others decide to grow the selected crop. Along with most producers, tree and nut crop growers would probably emphasize that if development is not economically sustainable then it is not sustainable.

However, growers need also to recognise that community as a whole looks at sustainability from a broader perspective: they are not only interested in the continued availability of a valued product, but are also concerned about the environmental, economic and social impacts of horticultural production beyond the farm gate.

Three major educational needs emerge from producers' increased recognition of the importance of sustainability, and the differing perspectives of producers and rest of society in considering sustainability issues.

These are:

1. The need for those in the industry (and those entering it) to understand how to manage their land and water resources for sustainable production and how to obtain acceptable returns at the same time as protecting the resources
2. The need for those in the industry to understand community expectations of sustainable development
3. The need for community to learn about horticultural issues in ways that encourage their participation in reaching sustainable solutions.

This paper identifies the broader expectations of sustainable development, suggests some educational principles for sustainability in horticulture, and provides examples of initiatives that might be useful models for education programs.

Issues in Sustainable Development for Horticulture

From the producers' viewpoint, specific issues threatening the sustainability of tree and nut cropping vary from place to place. Some geographically specific examples are salinity in the orchard crops of the Murray River basin, and soil erosion in sloping plantations of Queensland and northern New South Wales. Widespread issues include nutrient and pesticide contamination of waterways adjacent to orchards and limited supplies of water. There are undoubtedly other important issues (both environmental and economic) which can best be identified by those in the industry. Less obvious and perhaps as yet unknown issues may arise through major environmental changes such as global warming.

The issues of developing sustainable farming systems and having quality assurance protocols adopted by growers affect horticulture as well as other rural industries. To identify these issues from society's perspective, it is appropriate to look at the broad dimensions of the concept of ecologically sustainable development (ESD). While there is a lack of general agreement on its precise definition-there are, in fact, more than 160 documented definitions (McLeod 1993)-a set of principles has emerged from deliberations in 1987 by the World Commission on Environment and Development, and subsequent debate, including documentation of the Australian Government's interpretation of ESD.

The following principles (underlined) are adaptations (Department of Education, Queensland 1992, p. 9) of principles identified in the discussion paper *Ecologically Sustainable Development* (1990). Alongside each principle, we offer an interpretation for horticulturists.

Principles for the Physical Environment

- Limited natural resource use: Avoid wasting resources through over-production
- Efficient use of resources: Keep within the capability limits of the land and water
- Preservation of natural capital: Look after the soil and water
- Conservation of biodiversity: Don't break the chain that maintains a healthy living environment
- Precautionary policies: Be cautious not cavalier introducing new technology

Economic Principles

- Resilience: Avoid vulnerability to external disruptions-plan ahead and diversify
- Pricing policies: Recognise the value of natural resources and cover the costs of using them
- Balance: This refers to a balanced external economy to avoid excess pressure on natural capital; perhaps it applies at the farm level as well

Social Principles

- Community participation: Involve community in decisions about sustainable use
- Social equity: Consider whether new technology adversely affects other people's livelihood, or treats people unfairly
- Global perspective: Consider whether development in one place will cause social problems elsewhere
- Qualitative development: Consider factors like health and lifestyle which are benefits of development, as well as dollar returns
- Intergenerational equity: Leave the next generation with an environment that is at least as healthy, diverse and productive as is enjoyed today

It might be asking a lot to expect horticulturists to bear all of these principles in mind when planning a new venture. Nevertheless, an educational program for sustainable horticulture needs to help producers understand how society views sustainable development and assist them to make wise decisions in the light of that understanding. At the same time it needs to lead community to an appreciation of horticultural issues and a reasonableness in what it expects of sustainable horticulture.

An Appropriate Educational Program

An educational program dealing with sustainability issues aims for awareness, understanding of issues, attitudes that lead to commitment, and ultimately action for sustainability (Fien 1993).

Education for sustainability needs to be based in practical experiences and have an intention to do something; it is not an academic exercise. This message is highlighted by environmental educators who plan around the concept that environmental education is ABOUT (understanding how the system works and identifying the potential impact of activities); IN (providing practical experience; gathering data and making field assessment) and FOR the environment (developing skills to improve, and willingness to act).

The emphasis may differ for producers and community members. For instance, the focus for producers may be to enable them to feel confident in making personal decisions that are both sustainable and profitable. For some community members, awareness of the issues facing horticulture and efforts to move towards sustainability might be sufficient. Others, however, will want to be involved in a process that enables them to assess the issues and collaborate in decision-making.

Having identified the appropriate aims it is important to use delivery methods that suit the various interest groups.

For producers, short informal workshops may be more practical and acceptable than courses, even though the learning may be more disjointed. For potential producers the principles can be established in formal training by building appropriate sustainable management education into degree and TAFE courses in horticulture. This should follow a general appreciation of sustainability issues developed through the school curricula. For other community members, delivery is needed at two levels-awareness-raising activities and publicity will suit some, while others need to be offered hands-on participation in assessing issues and finding solutions.

Education Methods for Producers

There seems to be an in-built resistance by many experienced farmers to any suggestion of 'education' or training. Industry leaders and the rural press have commented frequently on this. The following editorial comment for the *Australian Rural Times*, 15-21 February 1990, provides just one example:

National Farmers Federation president John Allright put it squarely when he said that unless farmers gave education a higher priority they would condemn themselves and their industries to inevitable decline and non-viability.

Those running rural courses have identified several reasons for non-participation:

- Farmers don't like exposing their deficiencies in a group situation
- Many don't feel comfortable attending an educational institution and don't like the way courses are presented
- Farmers are concerned about the time and cost
- Many farmers are only willing to go to a course when nothing is happening on the farm: they don't plan for it

- While 'doing another course' is well accepted in the city, it is not yet well accepted in the country (Keith & Bryant ,1992).

For their part, producers might reply that what is offered doesn't contain what they want, and they would respond to courses tailored to their needs.

However, there are indications that this reluctance to take advantage of training/education opportunities is waning. Responsibilities being thrust upon or taken up by producers to be self-reliant information seekers (partly through changes in government extension services), and more appealing alternative methods now emerging suggest that farmers will soon make better use of education opportunities.

Educational approaches for sustainable management that are currently working or being put in place include:

Property Management Planning Workshops : Property management planning offers an opportunity to integrate the capability and management requirements of natural resources with production technology, enterprise potential, and the financial and personal goals of the farm family. In Queensland for example, a wide range of short (usually one day) modules are available or being developed to allow producers to begin at their point of initial interest, and then move into other areas pertinent to the development of their own enterprise. Workshops previously provided on soils, landuse, water quality and similar issues in an ad hoc way are being placed in their appropriate context within the whole umbrella of property management planning.

Shared learning through landcare groups : Productivity discussion groups have been around for a long time. Many landcare groups offer similar opportunities to share experience, with an emphasis on sustainable management. As well as workshops run by extension agencies based on priorities set by the landcare groups, producers visit each other's properties to discuss management options for various situations. This does require a willingness to reveal the 'warts' as well as show off the positive actions.

The group can also be a powerful forum for drawing together information of common interest from outside, and undertaking monitoring of various parameters that affect sustainable management, such as organic matter levels, soil compaction, pH or insect build-up.

GRASS Check (Forge 1994) is an example of a package developed to support this type of activity that is now being well used. Landholders who are interested in monitoring the condition of their native pastures, attend a group training day, receive a manual and then establish several monitoring sites on their property. They then periodically record data on the tests of interest to themselves or the group. The group can then meet at a later stage to discuss findings. This principle could be used for tree and nut crop related issues to generate data for shared learning. *GRASS Check* has a companion, *Soil Check*, which is designed for soil monitoring under any land use.

Action research methods such as Waterwatch and Saltwatch described in the section on community education are also useful tools to increase understanding by landusers.

Farmer participatory research : Both internationally and in Australia, sustainable farming systems are being developed through collaborative learning by researchers, extension workers and growers conducting on-farm experiments. In this way growers, ho are best placed to see the problems and carry out the crop management, link with the scientific insights and measuring processes provided by agency staff. This allows the participatory action research cycle of planning, action, observation and reflection to be applied in ways that quickly identify the best practices.

Modular courses : It is now becoming easier to take small 'bite-sized' chunks of education courses. Formal courses through TAFE and other institutions are now being presented in module form: units that provide their own set of learning outcomes which can be linked with others to build up a whole course, or else taken as 'one-off' learning activities by those with special interest in the topic. This gives the flexibility that producers often need, allowing useful topics to be taken without doing a full course. One such course developed in Western Australia for use by TAFE nationally includes topics on monitoring and managing soils, managing water (including irrigation) and waterways, and managing organic systems. It might be useful to add a fruit tree and nut crop management module to this. Landcare modules have also been built into some TAFE horticulture courses.

- Another useful development is the increasing ability to enter courses such as these through 'recognition of prior learning' in which experience counts rather than necessarily having to have a formal pre-qualification.
- *Continuing education short courses* TAFE and other institutions, in fierce competition for education dollars, provide a myriad of short courses for both beginners and advanced practitioners. Horticulture has a place in these courses, and sustainable management needs to be added as an adjunct to that. Resource materials already developed such as *Self-help Landcare for New Farmers* (Jordan, 1993), *Buying the Farm for Horticulture: Site it Right* (Carr 1986) and an AGRI-LINK package (*Looking after your Horticultural Land,* 1994), provide almost ready-made foundations for short, interesting courses in sustainable management for horticulture.

New self-help information collection systems : The age of videos, computer networks such as Internet and Landcare net, CD-ROMs, hotline faxes and decision support software has arrived. While uptake of some of these has been slower than expected, the momentum is bound to increase rapidly and suddenly everyone will be doing it (perhaps a 10-year goal). Information nodes such as Community Telecentres being tried by the Commonwealth Government and Information Centres similar to those being set up by Queensland Department of Primary Industries provide help with accessing these systems. It is important that research on sustainable methods by industry and government scientists be fed into these self-help collection systems.

Education Methods for Community

Education about, in and for sustainable development is best achieved by participative learning processes: participative in the sense that people are actively taking part in collecting information and also in the sense that people interact to share information and reach collective conclusions. There is much more to participative research than merely collecting and sharing information. There is a complex mix of 'synthesizing and recording, analysing and planning, belonging and experiencing, committing and acting, evaluating and communicating' (Kelly 1995, p. 102).

Saltwatch, focusing on salinity, and Waterwatch, a water quality monitoring program are two such participative educational programs relevant to sustainable horticulture issues. Other 'watch' programs focusing on beetles, worms, pasture, etc. follow comparable action research processes and could serve as models for exploring various facets of sustainable horticulture.

Salinity issues in Victoria, which have an impact on tree horticulture, sparked some innovative information collection and educational programs which have been further developed in other States. Saltwatch was the prototype. Students collect water samples from known sources, test salinity, transmit the salinity values and grid references to research centres by computer disk, and in return receive a district map setting out the readings. This can be used as a discussion point with the local landcare group.

A related issue, depth of watertable, gave rise to 'Watertable Watch' in some fruit growing areas of Victoria.

A simple method for students and community members to trace changes in the watertable was devised and used to manage water usage.

Waterwatch (along with companion concepts Streamwatch, and Ribbons of Blue), is a more complex program. It covers a range of physical, chemical and biological tests for water quality and streambank condition. Waterwatch generates an understanding of catchment issues by linking data from schools, community groups, individual landusers and perhaps local government authorities throughout a catchment. It is important to note that it is a valuable meeting point for producers with the rest of community, and interactions provide opportunities to share perceptions and values as well as data, and to collaborate in developing workable solutions to catchment issues. The Waterwatch approach was based on work done several years ago by the University of Michigan with a local river catchment community (Mitchell & Stapp 1995).

While these programs provide a sound basis for learning about catchment issues and developing rapport between producers and other community members, industry could supplement these with programs more specifically focused on horticulture.

Another aspect of an effective educational program is to match resources to school curricula, so that teachers are given the opportunity to use them to meet their own teaching objectives. This involves the important step of alerting teachers to these opportunities and, if needed, providing training (this is done with Saltwatch and Waterwatch programs). In developing educational resources for schools, it is important to liaise with curriculum developers at an early stage.

AMERICAN HORTICULTURAL SOCIETY

The American Horticultural Society (AHS) is one of the oldest national gardening organizations in the country. Since

1922, we have provided America's gardeners with the highest quality gardening and horticultural education possible. We accomplish this with the help of an impressive network of experts — from the members of our Board of Directors, specialized Advisory Committees, National Great American Gardener Award Winners and corporate sponsors. At AHS you'll get connected — to great gardens around the world, gardening education for all levels of skill, sources of information on any garden subject imaginable, a community of gardeners eager to share their experiences, other great gardening events and activities, and much, much more.

Social Impacts of Climate Change on Horticulture Tourism

The situation for many in Horticulture as a result of the current drought (particularly in, but not limited to, the deepening crisis in the lower Murray Darling Basin) has resulted in an unprecedented process of unplanned structural adjustment on a massive scale.

Drought is an inherent part of agriculture in Australia.

Consequences of drought directly impact on growers, farming families, local businesses and regional communities. Horticulture is inextricably linked with the economic, social and cultural vigour and sustainability of significant numbers of regional communities spread widely across the country. It is not possible to clearly separate economic sustainability of producers and regions from the social impacts on those regions and communities, and the multiplier for horticulture is estimated, on average, as a factor of five.

For the first time ever horticulture producers across the country have been seriously impacted by this drought. This has resulted in outcomes that are outside those usually experienced by farming operations and the communities that support them. Horticultural production units are far more intensive than broadacre operations, and are in the main irrigated. The impacts of drought on perennial plantings have been devastating. As large labour users, the resultant business consequences have been dire not just for our growers, but also for the communities which rely on them as key economic drivers.

As Cyclone Larry's impact on north Queensland's communities or the deepening crisis in the MDB amply illustrate, it is not possible to view economic or social consequences of drought or disaster in isolation.

In March 2009, the Victorian Department of Sustainability and Environment's executive director (Campbell Fitzpatrick) reported that the Victorian towns located along the Murray that are irrigation-dependant - such as Mildura and Swan Hill - will be impacted significantly by climate change, through the removal of water from those locations. This human aspect of climate change, already a reality in South Australia's Riverland, is a real risk for horticulture and the significant regional and rural communities it supports.

Impacts on Health and Well-being

The emotional toll on growers, their families and communities of climate change impacts to date (such as increased incidence of drought and reduced water availability), is increasing for horticultural businesses which have a large investment in their irrigation-reliant cropping system.

The low irrigation allocations have created a level of uncertainty throughout the industry; and changing allocations and inconsistencies between regions do not provide growers with the confidence in their water security. Some families have increasingly needed to seek off-farm income to remain viable. The WinHort (Women in Horticulture) Network no longer exists nationally, but some attempts have been made to enable local networking and encourage growers to socialize and share their issues in a casual setting. However, this local movement is not always successful as people under stress tend to withdraw.

Uncertainty, increasing workloads and increasing debt all contribute to the stress of growers. This will have significant impact on future communities, employment in rural areas, and the health and well-being of those current members of the industry.

CHAPTER–10

HORTICULTURAL TOURISM MARKETING

Tourists makeup the third, and perhaps most important subsystem. Successful tourism programs require a strong market orientation. The needs and wants of the tourists you choose to attract and serve must be the focus of much of your marketing and development activity. Therefore, it is important to clearly understand which tourism market segments you wish to attract and serve. Tourists fall into a very diverse set

of categories with quite distinct needs and wants. You should identify the different types of tourists, or market segments that you presently serve or would like to serve. This may involve one or more tourism market surveys.

Having understood the current profile of Indian tourism, it is possible to analyse the marketing efforts put in by the Department of Tourism, Government of India. While starting tourism promotion in a modest way in the early fifties, the Government of India had no clear-cut objectives and goals about how to go about it. Tourism promotion was considered an information service like information on any other aspect of a country i.e. trade, economy, etc. Nothing more.

To most government officials involved in tourism promotion in the early fifties, international tourism meant that some affluent people from rich countries with a lot of money and some curiosity (especially from the US) were willing to travel to foreign lands. It was recognised that the first preference of such people in North America would be Europe which they considered the cradle of Western civilisation. However, the retired and more affluent among them could be persuaded to take round-the-world trips either by ship or by air which sometimes included India. That was the India's target group in the fifties and sixties.

In North America, or for that matter in the entire Western world, India, if known at all, at that time had the image primarily of an exotic country — hot and humid, poor and backward, a land of snake charmers and rope walkers — an image which the British authors like Kipling had built up over the decades. The British rulers projected this image as they had to stand the heat of long summers in India to administer the country. Their families retired to the hills with cooks, bearers, nannies and gardeners and there was little attempt at meeting the people of India and understanding their rich culture.

In the early fifties, the government decided that India should have overseas offices to project a new image of the country as a tourist destination. The markets chosen were the USA, the UK followed by West Germany, France and Australia. These offices were essentially information offices whose job was to distribute and disseminate tourist information through brochures printed in India. In an effort to do everything in India, they forgot that their publicity material exported out of India was not attractive enough and of the best quality.

Although these offices were useful in projecting the new image of an independent India, some of the offices were perhaps opened a little too soon. For instance, an India tourist office was opened in Germany in 1957 at a time when the Germans had just undertaken travelling outside their country. They were not ready for India. It took them a decade before they began taking long distance holiday trips to countries like India and that too only when holidays to India became relatively inexpensive due to the introduction of charters and the cheaper inclusive group fares on scheduled carriers. Similarly, India opened a tourist office in Japan in 1964, when Japan first liberalised its foreign exchange restrictions and allowed the Japanese to take only three hundred dollars for travel overseas. But traffic from Japan to India remained static for five years as the Japanese did not think beyond the USA and Europe as their preferred holiday or business destinations. In Australia also, the story was more or less repeated as Australians started taking India holidays or stopovers on the way to Europe only in the early seventies. However, these tourist offices were useful in paving the way for tourism from these markets in later decades.

Modest advertising campaigns were launched by the tourist offices overseas within their limited resources. It was generally a well thought out activity undertaken on the advice of the professional advertising agencies hired by each tourist office locally to improve the image of India as a land of Ajanta-Ellora, the Taj Mahal, the Himalayas and Mahabalipuram. Cultural tourism relating to monuments and an ancient civilisation was the initial thrust of promotion as people in the Western world could more readily identify India with such an image. The frequency and the size of advertisements was inadequate. Advertisements were released mostly in black and white as colour advertising was considered too expensive. At the same time, tourist offices, however, established contacts with the tour-operators and travel agents to persuade them to send their clients to India.

Concept of Tourism Marketing

Marketing is a human activity. All the activities of tourism marketing bear a glaring testimony to this fact. In tourism marketing, we deal with mobile, enthusiastic and pleasure-seeking humans. They are on travel sprees. They want to enjoy the nice places of the world! They are efficient (at least during the courses of their journeys), conscious of the environs they visit, always careful about the money they spend, keen to explore and receptive to every phenomenon/ product/service that makes comfortable or ecstatic.

We have defined Marketing in this chapter. Let us now define the term Tourism Marketing. According to Krippendorf, "Marketing in tourism is to be understood as the, systematic and co-ordinated execution of business policy by a tourist undertaking, whether private_ or State, owned at local, regional, national and international levels, to achieve the optimal satisfaction of the needs of identifiable consumer groups and in doing so, achieves an appropriate return."

According to Burkart and Medlick, "Tourism marketing activities are systematic and coordinated efforts extended by the National Tourist Organisation and/or tourists at local levels to optimise the satisfaction of tourist groups and individuals in view of sustained tourism growth."

According to A Kumar, "Tourism marketing is the delineation and execution of activities related to tourism their professional planning and execution and finally, ensuring the satisfaction of customers (tourists) in such a manner that the marketing objectives of the tourism organisation are achieved within the framework of social, economic, political and environmental components of the place/region/country of origin as well as that of the place/region/country of tour destination."

Thus, we can arrive at some conclusions regarding tourism marketing, as follows :-

(A) Tourism marketing is the process of delivering satisfaction to tourists and in this process, the tourism marketer achieve his personal goals or the goals of the firm he works for.

(B) Tourism marketing is a service-based activity. Some parts of its realm are products, some of them (like food beverages etc.) being very important.

(C) Just like other types of marketing, tourism marketing also involves:

Strategic Planning (which includes definition of business mission, corporate strategic planning, business strategic planning, goal formulation definition of a marketing plan, finalization of marketing programmes, implementation of marketing programmes and finally, receipt of feedback and control);

Analysis of Marketing Opportunities (which includes marketing research, study of marketing environment, study of consumer behaviour and finally, study of competition);

Selection of Targeted Markets (which includes forecasting market demand, defining market segments, making plans for market targeting and finally, product positioning);

Design of Appropriate Marketing Strategies (which includes definition and identification of market leaders, challengers, followers and niches, defining the PLC of the product and using this knowledge to create market niches for the product/service and finally, understanding the intricacies of import and export management);

Planning Marketing Programmes (which includes definition and management of product lines and brands, development and testing of new products, brand management, marketing of services, pricing policies and discounts, definition and consolidation of marketing channels, study and consolidation of physical distribution channels, making effective promotion strategies, defining sales promotion and public relations programmes and finally, management of the sales force);

Implementing Marketing Programmes (which includes study/creation of a marketing organisation and implementation of marketing programmes in targeted market niches); and.

Controlling (which includes various types of control systems in the parlance of marketing).

1. It is a process of transforming potential customers (tourists) into actual customers.
2. It is a fine technique for generating and consolidating tourism demand.
3. It can be used to increase market share of the tourism marketer.
4. It essentially uses the tenets of communication, business management and psychology to win the markets in the parlance of tourism administration.
5. It deals with human beings most of the times; they are the customers with very special and weird needs. Most of them indulge in activities related to tourism due to the fact that they want to enjoy. This peculiar feature of tourism marketing makes it special. It also demands different marketing strategies to woo the customers towards the products and services that are offered to them.
6. Tourism packages, Group inclusive Tours, economy package deals and luxury packages area part of the gamut of tourism marketing.
7. It involves many services or products of the infrastructure of a region or country. This makes it a Herculean effort; without making right types of teams, a tourism marketer cannot succeed in this effort.
8. Tourism marketing starts from implementation of local or regional programmes but eventually, all the marketers try (or dream) to win international market hitches which were hitherto beyond their reach.

Tourism is predominantly a service. It involves many people (tourists, tour operators, transporters, hotel staff, guides, restaurant staff, disk jockeys etc.). It is of perishable nature.

The unique features of tourism demand are as follows :-

(a) It is perishable by nature.

(b) The demand is more during peak seasons and very low during off seasons.

(c) Tourists demand products and services of different kinds from the producers of the same set of tourism services or products. But they have to produce all such types of these services or product to remain competitive in the markets.

(d) Demand for luxury products and services is low. Demand for low-end services and product is very high.

(e) Some tourists, who may be belonging to middle-income strata of the society, may try to touch, albeit occasionally, the luxury norms of the strata that are above their strata.

(f) For some tourist spots, the demand is more or less inelastic. But for others, it is elastic.

As already stated, tourism is a service. It comprises some products as well. These include food, liquor, beverages, gifts, souvenirs, items, of daily use etc. But basically, the tourist (customer) buys services while he takes up a tour or itinerary. Example: One cannot expect a tourist to go to Mauritius to buy a few items that are typical to that country. He travels to that country to enjoy her environs, swim in the blue waters of the ocean, stay at exotic places and have a glimpse of the coral reefs that are under the waters of the ocean. He may or may not buy gifts or souvenirs, though he would certainly eat the cuisine of Mauritius.

Now that we are clear about the tenet that tourism is a service, we would have to weave a strategy set to bring customers to our fold. Service marketing is different from product marketing. It is intangible; the tourist cannot consume a tourist spot can only enjoy its environs. When he goes back to his native place, he takes sweet memories along with him. The tourism product is, therefore, essentially associated with 3 features, as follows: -

(A) Perceptions in the mind of the tourist-to-be about the tourist spot, including his expectations and a portrayal of what is in store for him.

(B) The actual experiences (good or bad) of the tourist at the spot.

(C) Sweet memories (even bitter ones) that he takes back along with him to his native place.

If a customer tries a product and does not like it, he discards it. But if a tourist tries a tourist spot and does not like it, he cannot cancel his tour. This feature differentiates tourism (as a service) from other services and products. He cannot call it a day in the middle of the journey because he was offered beef and pork by the hotel! He has to drag on somehow. Our advice to the tourism marketer is-do not let the tourist have the feeling of dragging on; eliminate this feeling as soon as it develops in his mind. If you don't, he would not give a good word-of-mouth about your tourist spot or service to others. You would lose him as well as scores of other tourists who could have become your customers, had he been treated nicely to kill that feeling of dragging on.

Further, tourism, as a service, is given only when political stability of the region is ensured.

Instance: Kashmir is a paradise on the earth but not a hot spot for tourists because of the supremacy of terrorists in that valley. A tourist does not like the hullabaloo of crowd, rallies, riots, arson and instability. He wants to enjoy and relax at the tourist spot; he may have spent the savings of his return to undertake the trip. Every tourism organisation must understand this fact.

WELL PLANNED MARKETING

Market planning in the fifties and the sixties was not really feasible because the base of Indian tourism was narrow. The resources for promotion were even more limited and, tourism being a new industry, personnel were not well-trained.

For preparing any successful marketing plan, we deal with four variables, popularly known in the marketing jargon as the four Ps.

Product: It means attractions or tourist resources that a country can offer — beautiful monuments, scenic beauty, beach and mountain resorts, transportation services, good hotel accommodation, polite and friendly people, etc.

Price: It implies the optimal rates at which the tourism product (holiday) can be sold.

Place: Most suitable distribution channels. In other words, the markets where the product should be sold and the network through which it is sold.

Promotion: It implies the communication process, public relations, advertising, promotion, etc.

To begin with, the Indian tourist 'product' had several drawbacks. The major shortcoming was the image. India did not enjoy the image of a holiday destination.

Indians were often shocked to see the results of surveys conducted by organisations like PATA showing India in a terribly bad light. Despite the shock the fact remained that India had an image problem about its tourist product everywhere, especially in the USA. The picture in Western Europe was not very different. In 1961, the London Observer questioned its readers where they were planning to spend their holidays in 1962. India was not even mentioned among the first twelve popular destinations. A member of the Indian Parliament on return from England in 1966 quoted a placard shown in London which read:

Positive news came from Germany. In a survey carried out in the Federal Republic of Germany, the respondents were asked in the early sixties: 'If you could do as you liked, where would you go and what would you like to see and do most of all'? They were given the choice of twenty two places and activities; for example:

The Egyptian Pyramids

The ruins of ancient Greece

The skyscrapers of New York

The Kremlin in Moscow

The Hollywood film studios

A journey across the ocean in a sailing ship

To watch a nuclear explosion

The Isle of Capri

Paris

St. Peter's in Rome

Tour to India

Surprisingly, India was the most popular country outside the European continent.

The image problem was further complicated by the inadequacy of transport and hotel accommodation, both in quality and quantity. In 1967, the Director of the Government of India tourist office in San Francisco called on a major travel agency and the following conversation took place with the President of the company, with the President doing the most of the talking.

"Sir you have beautiful, colourful literature on India. I must compliment you on its production."

"Thank you very much. How is the business?"

"You have a great country with varied tourist attractions."

"Thank you again for saying that."

"You have a very nicely located office in a central place in San Francisco. Your staff is polite and efficient."

"Well you are making my day...."

"But, Sir, why don't you close down your office?"

"Now, tell me, why do you say that after paying me all these compliments this morning?"

"Better buy some planes for Indian Airlines for tourists. I cannot get confirmation on Indian Airlines for my clients for months. How can I sell India?" he asked. "Presently, what you need is capacity on Indian Airlines and not promotion. Close your shop and go back home," he advised.

This was duly reported to the Government of India, but the government had its own priorities. It was a time when Indian Airlines had not bought its Boeings and Airbuses, and the capacity on most routes was limited.

No amount of marketing and promotion could help India with these constraints.

The Indian Airlines' capacity was increased in December 1970 when Boeing 737s were bought; later their fleet was augmented by the addition of more such planes and in 1988 and after by the purchase of 19 Airbuses. Despite these purchases, Indian Airlines' capacity did not catch up with the increasing demand. The situation is a little better today though popular tourist routes are still overcrowded during the season. By 1997, the Indian Airlines had more planes than pilots, and Indian Airlines fleet was underutilised—the other extreme.

The introduction of a Hotel Loan Development Fund in 1968 eased the accommodation situation somewhat. While marketing India's tourist product, price too was an important factor to be taken into consideration. Although India's tourist facilities were relatively inexpensive, the high airfares were a negative factor in the major tourist markets of the world. The majority of tourists to India come by air from long distances — an expensive way of travelling compared to road or rail travel as in Europe.

It would be seen that India's share in world tourism cannot be very large till there is a significant inter-regional movement. If the experience of other countries provides a clue, large-scale tourism cannot originate from long-distance markets. European countries and Canada, Mexico and the Carribbean receive a majority of their tourists from the neighbouring areas. East Asia — Thailand, Singapore, Hong Kong, the Philippines and Malaysia — receives a sizeable number of visitors from neighbouring countries. Till such time as India develops large-scale inter-regional traffic, it cannot have "mass tourism" or even tourism on a large-scale. Tense political relations and economic weaknesses of India's neighbours preclude any such possibility in the coming years.

Keeping in mind these factors, Indian advertising strategy in the sixties was essentially to tell American travellers they could break their journey in India on round-the-world tours, and to the Europeans that India was a home of a great civilisation, culture and architectural wonders. A market study conducted in the United States through the Stanford Research Institute in the early sixties revealed that Americans having an annual income of US $ 10,000 to 15,000 per year alone could afford to travel to India and in addition, only those who had a lot of intellectual curiosity. Indian advertising was, therefore, targeted to the people in this income bracket and among them also to those who had already travelled to Europe.

PRINCIPLES OF MARKETING

Marketing is essentially a human activity. It is a social science. The ultimate objective of a marketer is to develop an image in the minds of the target customers, which should enable them to buy your products and services for long periods of time. The products, services and methodologies for delivering them take a back-seat; what remains vital for the success of a business is the development and maintenance of healthy relationships with the targeted market niches. And that is not at all a difficult task if the firm in question completes its homework before undertaking actions to win its markets. Let us begin with some basic terms.

Human Beings : An individual is a human being who lives in the world according to the laws defined by nature. Humans are individuals but they are social beings as well, just like any other living species. Human beings are living, perceiving forms of life. They respond to stimuli of five types-vision, sound, touch, taste and smell. Humans are also keen to survive and grow. For many of them, however, growth in mental terms is more important than survival.

The Needs and Wants : A need is the state of felt deprivation of some basic satisfaction in an individual. Every human being has some needs. These needs vary from individual to individual. If, for example, a person is hungry, then food is his need. Hunger is a physiological process. Food would safety hunger of the individual. We are marketing our products, services and thoughts to humans. Every human being has set of needs.

The need set of every person varies but we can classify the same, for our convenience, into 5 broad categories. This classification was given by Henry Maslow. It is as follows:-

Basic : These are the physiological needs, like food, clothing, sex, shelter and other vital requirements for survival. These needs arise because of the very existence of man and he ought to satisfy them in order to thrive on this planet. Example: A young boy needs food immediately after his return from his school.

Security : These are the needs to be satisfied after the basic needs have been satisfied. These include the security of home, family and belongings. Every person wants to operate in a stable and terror—free environment. He wants to lie without any threats to his existence. The basic needs are satisfied easily (even by the poorest of people) but security needs demand more resource and physical efforts. Example: A person would like to keep his home secure by locking its main entrance, lest a thief should break into his house and take away his valuables, or harm his family members.

Social : Man is a social animal. He wants to move in the company of those people who are dear to him. Naturally, he would seek to be a part of only those groups in which, he is heard, valued and cared for. However, some people may not have social needs at all; they might love to remain in the secluded corners of their homes or offices. In general, however, man expects to remain in a pleasant company. Example: An elder person may not like to go home for most of the time and remain in the temple where he prays. At home, he might be feeling out of place as nobody might be giving ample time (and attention) that may be due to him. The company of his friends (who are mostly elders of his age group) might be a blessing for him.

Ego : Every person has an ego set. If his ego set is offended, he retaliates (through words, gestures or even through physical actions). He takes pride in some activities and would like to be known because of them. Ego is an essential ingredient of man and he cannot be told to shun it. Self-esteem is a part of this set of needs. The meaning of both these terms is similar, with only a few minor variations. Example: An executive could have ego due to the fact that he has been authorised to purchase goods worth *US$ 27,000* for his firm.

Self-Actualisation : Every human being is a minute representation of the Almighty. God has sent him to this mortal world for carrying out some tasks. However, some tasks are related to the benefit of the mankind. Every person may not have an inkling of the needs of people and environment around him. A person with an activated self-actualisation need becomes a great person during his lifetime. He forgets about his basic needs and works for the masses. Examples: Gandhi, Martin Luther King, Mother Teresa etc.

The needs of people vary and most of them continue to struggle for satisfying them. Therefore, it is the duty of an entrepreneur to keep a tab on the needs of people in its targeted market segments. He would have to keep in regular touch with them, read text about them in the print media, listen to their demands and complaints and above all, be sympathetic towards them while trying to sell his products and services to them. Successful marketers are those who can create the needs for those products and services, which the target customers might not require. It is a difficult task but proper understanding of the buyer behaviour and meticulous planning of marketing efforts could deliver coveted results for the marketer.

Henry Maslow had pointed out that these needs were satisfied by an individual in the order described above. However, many exceptions to this order have been found in the annals of history, which indicate that these needs may not be proponent in an individual in this order. It also gives such examples related to tourism administration as are related to the needs defined by Maslow.

At one time, only one need is proponent in the mind of an individual. A child cannot ask for food and at the same time, demand a bicycle. First of all, he may take the bicycle and have fun with his friends. After his return, he may bother his mother for food. You must keep this basic concept in mind. The most proponent need of the prospective customer must be satisfied first. After satisfying that need, the very next need in the order of importance is to be satisfied. If the order dictated by the customer or the prospective customer is disturbed, the marketing gimmick may fail and the marketer may end up wasting his precious time, money and other resources.

There is another important concept related to wants. All the needs may not be manifested in terms of wants. Someone (preferably, marketing or manufacturing firm) may have to convert a need into a want. If a need is converted into a want, then only that firm would be able to satisfy the need of that particular customer. If the firm becomes a pioneer in terms of converting a need into a want, it could become one of the most successful entrepreneurs the mankind may have ever seen! How, for example, the want for a cellular phone was generated around the world? In fact, there was a need for communicating while being on the move and the executive, housewife or any person could not have waited to stand in a queue and call through a public call office. The element of grace and "high- end" was attached later to the cellular communication mode. The primary objective was to save time while moving (a primary need).

The secondary objective was to talk to the person (associated in business or at home) as and when the need arose (the secondary need). These twin objectives were achieved through a cellular phone (the want). The want was created in the markets of Europe through media blitzkrieg and exclusive features of cellular phones (the chief among them being the ability to talk while on the move). The cellular mania took the European markets by storm during the early eighties as a result of the excruciating marketing efforts of Siemens, AirTel, Nokia, Samsung and Panasonic. This war of nerves still goes on in the emerging markets of Asia. Can we create the need for such products also as are not required by the human race? The marketer need not work hard to create the need for tobacco, alcohol and other vices. But if we answer the aforementioned question in the negative, then the marketer would state, "My uncle is in liquor business and he is the best person in the entire world !" We would contend that no business is bad.

However, while choosing a business stream, we would have to take into account our educational background, the reputation of our parents, financial resources available, suggestions of our friends and relatives and above all, our abilities (as well as limitations). You cannot jump into the liquor business simply because there is a great demand for liquor or because our uncle has been successful in this business. Further, we know that liquor consumption is bad for health. We would have to give a serious thought to acceptance of our products and services by the society in the light of legal, environmental and broad societal constraints in which, it thrives. Example: The need of a person is hunger. He can satisfy his need by consuming a burger. So, his want is a burger. The firm that manufactures burgers can deliver a message in the targeted markets (which would reach that hungry person) that burgers can satisfy the hunger of a hungry man. So, instead of consuming bread, *chapati*, lentils or vegetables, the hungry man can eat burgers (want) to satiate his hunger (need).

We would like to come back to the concept of wants. We want to satisfy the needs of the targeted markets through the products or services demanded by them (the wants). And just like new needs can be created, new wants can also be created among the targeted market niches. We can get an edge over our competitors by creating a different want for satisfying the same need of our customers. Example: We can sell cola drinks and beat the competition who might be selling orange drinks. The need remains the same-thirst. The wants (of buyers) would change-from orange drink (sold by the competitor) to cola drink (sold by us).

Types of Demands : Demand is a want for a specific product that is backed up by an ability and willingness to buy it. Example: If hunger is the need and burger is the want, then the demand of the person in question could be McDonald's Burger.

Demand can be of 4 types, as follows :—

Actual : It is that real demand that can be calculated by judging the past trends of the market. It is the demand for a product or service (in a given market niche) according to the current trends. There will be only minor changes in this demand, if we extrapolate the trends of the past into the future.

Latent : It is the demand that can be satisfied in future but is not known even to the targeted market niches.

New : It is the demand that can be created with respect of new products and services. These products and services have not arrived in the market as yet. But the demand for the same would have to be created first and then, these would have to be supplied to the targeted markets.

Negative : It is the demand for those products that the customer does not need. Rather, he shuns the use of such products. The demand for some of these products ought to be created in the interest of the welfare of a community or society. Examples: Family planning programmes, insurance policies.

***Satisfaction of Need* :** A product is something that can satisfy a need or want. All the products deliver services. A shaving blade is of no use unless it cleans the stubble of a man. A transport fleet is useless if it does not deliver the goods of a client in time.

Products are of many types and varieties. The buyers of these products try to buy those very products that can satisfy their actual needs. They may not be keen to buy those products that do not satisfy their needs or those that do not seem to be satisfying their needs. Products and services are available from the markets of the world. But only those products and services would be sold to the clients that meet their needs. The desperate seller of such goods and services may make efforts to create needs of products and services to garner profits' for his enterprise. In that event, needs are created. Such needs lead to wants. These wants, in turn, lead to demand. This is the most glaring feature of business operations going) around the globe.

You can satisfy the needs of the customers, which eventually become wants, through the products and services manufactured and sold by you. We would also include thoughts (or concepts) in this set. Religious affiliation with a temple or church is basically a thought. However, products and services are also important.

Products and services satisfy the needs of a person. Both of them deliver services—tangible and intangible. The marketer would be required to understand their needs and judge whether their wants are matching their needs or not (they might be wrong as well). After clearly understanding what the target markets want, the marketer should create such products or services as could satisfy these needs and wants. Products and services must be delivered at the right time, in the right quantity, with the right package and at the right place to the customer-to-be.

Profit Oriented Marketing

The objective of the marketing objective is to help the firms of the new millennium achieve their objectives. It refers to aim of the firm to make profits by executing the marketing tasks. Non-profit firms, government departments and NGOs could have the objectives of survival, good image, perfection, a place in the society etc. The profit-oriented firm identifies such opportunities in targeted market niches as can help it earn profits.

Problems of Market Oriented Firm : When the firm goes through the painful process of becoming a market-oriented company, it faces 3 problems-organised resistance, slow learning and fast forgetting. Organised resistance refers to opposition offered by other departments of the firm to the marketing department. Marketers counter such machinations by stating that the focus of the firm is the customer and not the marketing department. True, it is vital for understanding the needs of the customer and that is why, it assumes a key role in the firm, they contend.

The second issue is related to slow learning. The top brass supports the marketing function. Marketing professionals are hired from outside. Marketers are introduced to new marketing techniques through seminars. Budgets are increased. Planning and control systems are introduced. Thus, the function of marketing passes through:

(a) adver*tising, sales promotion and publicity; to*

(b) a friendly atmosphere; to

(c) innovation; to

(d) positioning; to

(e) analysis, planning and control.

The third and final issue is related to fast forgetting. The aforementioned five phases (in slow learning) tend to make the firm forget basic marketing principles. Success in markets makes the firm whimsical and it losses its focus, which is the need set of the targeted markets. So, there is a need to target the customer and not the products of the firm.

Concept of Societal Marketing

According to Kotler, "The societal marketing concept holds that the organisation's task is to determine the needs, wants and interests of target markets and to deliver the desired satisfaction more effectively and efficiently than competitors in a way that preserves, or enhances the consumer's and the society's well-being."

The issues related to global warming, societal development, protection of environment and human side of marketing are addressed in this concept. Three factors rule the minds of societal Marketers Company Profits, Consumer Want Satisfaction and Public Interest. Interests of backward groups, poor classes, ecology and society at large cannot be ignored while the firm satisfies the needs of its target markets to mint millions. This concept has assumed great importance in the wake of the operations of the free market system. Social responsibilities of business that were hither to dormant or of academic nature now guide the marketing policies and programmes of the firm. The organisation is a part of a society, environmental system and a well-defined group of humans, fauna and flora it cannot ignore the SOS calls of the elements of society and environment in which, it thrives simply because it is satisfying the needs of its markets (to earn profits)

Economic Significance : Marketing is the creation of a standard of living. It creates the demand for new products. It also satisfies dearly definable needs of customers. Thus, the process of marketing leads to customer satisfaction. It also generates an environment in which, other economic and social activities can be carried out. It enhances the ambition peaks of people and persuades them to work harder (so that they could buy new innovative products and services). Hence, marketing is a unique motivating force. It creates new sets of demand and satisfies old sets of demand. It is the lifeline of a society or nation. It helps people earn and spend to a much larger extent than before. It improves the economic status of an individual or family because he or it tries to emulate the buying habits of the economic level next to his or its level. Thus, marketing triggers various activities in a society, region or nation that ultimately lead to its economic progress.

Marketing Vital for Business Firm : At this juncture, it would be appropriate to point out that all the functional departments of the firm, namely, personnel, production, MIS and finance, are given a back-seat in the gamut of operations of the firm. Be all and end all of business is marketing. It creates a standard of living. The economic growth of a nation depends upon the strength of its marketing activities and the achievements of its hard-core marketing professionals. We do not ignore other functions either: However, if the perpetuation of a business is to be ensured, marketing activities ought to be given preference over all others.

Further, in the parlance of tourism administration, marketing assumes a much vital role. That is because operations of most of the tour operators and travel agencies are global or at least national. International marketing enters the gamut of operations of even small tourism organisations. Examples: All the travel agents must get accreditation from the IATA, if they wish to serve their customers on a national or global basis. Similarly, hotels must also have the approval or classification from the government, lest they should be treated as the *hoi polloi* of the hotel industry. Brand names work and sell in the tourism industry as well, just like they do in all other industries and businesses. Thus, the marketing department of a tour operator, airline, cruise line or hotel must build a brand image for itself through quality products and promotional tools.

MARKETING PROCESS

The first step in the marketing process is to carry out a Corporate Environment Analysis.

The Corporate Environment Analysis will list the company's corporate objectives, its strengths and weaknesses. It will also look into the financial environments under which the company will have to work during a given period.

The second step will be to identify the customers who will buy their products, where they live and what they want. This is called Market Research. Research may reveal that there is no point in advertising the beaches of India to Americans. They have enough of their own or in their neighbourhood—the Caribbean Islands. Northern Europe is India's best market for beach holidays because they do not have warm water beaches. And they are also geographically closer to India.

The third step is to look for the type of customers who will buy the product. Are your customers in the age group of 40-50 or do they come from the younger crowd? Are they professionals? Are they people who seek adventure or they are people looking for a cultural experience? Also who are the people who can afford your product? This is called Market Segmentation. We will, therefore, focus our promotion on the market we identify through this process.

The fourth step is Formulation of the Product. We formulate the product to suit each segment of our customers. The product must meet the needs of the customer.

The next step is Pricing. The company must price the product attractively to interest the customers. It should be affordable to customers we seek.

Distribution come next. Where do we sell our product, in which areas and through what kind of sales network? The product should be easily accessible to enable potential customers to buy it.

The next and most important part of the marketing process is to make sure that potential customers know about the product. It is called Promotion. It includes every aspect—mass-media, advertising, public relations, press releases, direct mail, etc., to draw the attention of customers to the product.

Tourism Services and Marketing

We shall discuss 3 types of marketing activities in this section-marketing of airlines, marketing of hotels and marketing of resorts.

Airlines and its Marketing : The basic task of an airline is the physical transportation of the client (tourist) to a tourist spot or a place that is closer to such a spot. The product/ service mix of an airline should be such as to achieve synchronisation of core and peripheral services. While providing core services, central transport of passengers and goods/cargo is done. While providing peripheral services, decent dealings of air hostesses, timely arrivals, timely departures, nice food aboard the aircraft On-flight catering), permission to consume liquor, hospitality of the airline etc are the factors to be pondered over.

The strategy for defining a marketing mix for the airlines industry should also include:

(a) banking;

(b) insurance;

(c) foreign ,exchange regulations;

(d) customs rules;

(e) declaration forms;

(f) various methods of airline promotion;

(g) various tools for promotion of air packages; and

(h) aviation safety issues.

Sophistication of technology (which involves aircraft maintenance, use of modern jet aircraft and supersonic craft), efficiency of passenger/cargo management (which involves fully automatic baggage handling systems) and an empathetic attitude for customers (which is a part of hospitality) are the factors for succeeding in the air travel business. But it is not easy to integrate these three factors to deliver concrete results. That is why, some airlines do not find customers for their aircraft services while some others remain booked throughout the year. Brand image also plays an important role in selling tickets air passengers. Airline transport business is vital for the country's economy; it also affects world economy.

Ideas of Product Mix

The following features are prominent :-

(a) It is an intangible product.

(b) Three major core services form a part of the product mix-passenger transport, cargo transport and mail transport.

(c) Expectations of customers must be matched with high quality of services. If this is not done, the airline can lose its vital market niches.

(d) Airlines operate in specific areas, called Sectors. Such sectors are created and covered according to the rules of the IATA, PATA, ICAO and other international organisations.

(e) Normally, the passenger service is of three types—Royal First Class, Royal Executive Class and Economy Class. These classes may be defined in a different manner by different airlines.

(f) Cargo management must go along with passenger transport. That is became the baggage of passengers must accompany them in the same aircraft. It must be loaded in the cargo much before the aircraft takes off.

(g) The USP of an airline is has 3 sub-USPs-transport by air at minimum costs, essential services to be given to the aircraft while the aircraft is airborne and movement of passengers to and from the aircraft. Flight data display is also a part of core services.

(h) Peripheral services are pleasant mannerisms (courtesy) of the aircrew, luxury levels inside the aircraft, music system, movies onboard the aircraft and above all, in-flight catering services. We can also include disaster management in the category of peripheral services.

Clearly, many persons are involved in giving services of various types to air passengers. Airport staff check documents of passengers. Airlines or their travel agents 'arrange tickets for them. Immigration officials check visas when the passengers arrive at least 2 hours *before* the departure of the aircraft. Transport officials (at the airport) receive the luggage and check it for the presence of any explosive/contraband items in the same. This procedure is carried out with the help of special machines. These machines scan each and every suitcase and bag. Then, these bags and suitcases are transferred to the luggage bay through an automatic conveyor belt. From that bay, transport vehicles (four wheelers) carry the luggage to the aircraft. The passengers move to departure terminals after they dear all the immigration formalities. They may have to pay airport taxes if the same have not been added to the ticket prices. Aboard the aircraft, passengers are welcomed by the airhostesses and shown their respective seats. These seats are mentioned on the boarding passes that are issued to passengers at the airport. Passengers are given fruit juice, light drinks, white wine, red wine or liquors when the aircraft becomes stable in the air. Beer is also served (in cans). Then, lunch or dinner is served by air hostesses. Information is displayed on the screen to give details of flight data. When the aircraft lands, passengers get up and leave the aircraft. The crew thank the passengers. At the destination airport, passengers get their passports and visas checked. Then, they proceed to collect their luggage, which arrives in the departure lounge through automatic conveyor belts. Every passenger is supposed to identify his or her luggage and pick it up from the conveyor belt as and when it arrives. Passengers put their luggage on wheeled trolleys and leave the airport. If the passenger has a tie-up with a travel agency, resort or hotel, the passenger is whisked away by a coach or taxi that represents that travel agency, resort or hotel.'

Ideas of Price Mix : The price of an air ticket comprises a basic fate and airport taxes, In addition, some airlines also impose a surcharge that is to be taken from passengers because of the rules and policies of a country. Sales tax is also a part of the bill. Nowadays, aviation turbine fuel costs, airport maintenance costs, aircraft costs and vacant seats have forced airlines to increase airfares of all the categories. This change varies from 5 to 15 *per cent* of the basic ticket cost. If a passenger or customer wishes to send cargo by air, he would have to get the goods booked at the airport. He would be issued an airway receipt, called Airway Bill. It is similar to a Railway Receipt (RR) in the case of rail transport or a Goods Receipt (GR) in the case of surface transport. The goods would be taken by air to the destination. The original document (airway bill) would have to be presented by the receiver at the destination airport so that he could get the delivery of goods. Obviously, the sender would send this receipt by courier, air or other method so that the receiver' is able to collect these goods. He would also be required to pay customs duty (if it is applicable) and other taxes that may be applicable from time to time for providing such services.

During off seasons and also during holiday seasons (May to July), airlines woo their customers by reducing airfares. This is a common practice followed by all the airlines of the world. Similarly, special incidents like the attacks on the WTC towers on September 11 ,2001 also force many airlines to cut down their prices. That is because the number of passengers falls rapidly in the wake of threats to passengers. They prefer to travel by sea or road due to these incidents. Thus, airlines reduce their fares so that passengers may continue to extend their patronage to them.

In order from the prices to be competitive, airlines must ensure that their seats do not go vacant when the aircraft is airborne. More the number of vacant seats, more would be the cost to passengers. If operational costs and landing charges at airports increase, airfares are bound to increase. Wars (like Iraq-US war in 2003), national calamities (like SARS in China, Hong Kong and Taiwan) and bad weather (like dust storms or fog at the IGI Airport) adversely affect smooth flow of air traffic. Rising price of Air Turbine Fuel (ATF) is also a deterrent in this context.

Air India and Indian Airlines have offered some lucrative schemes in the past to attract customers. **Example:** The IA had offered a ticket for *Rs 15,000* and allowed unlimited travel to any destination of India till March 31, 2003. The IA-Taj offer allows passengers to stay in any of the hotels of the Taj Group at an additional cost of *Rs 2,000.* Many other schemes are in vogue that persuade passengers to travel (at low costs).

Ideas of Promotion Mix

An airline can use the following components in rational combinations to define its promotion mix :—

Advertising: It can advertise through magazine, newspapers, local newspapers and on Internet to promote its products/services. Normally, travel agents do this job for the airlines. Airlines normally issue advertisements for image building in reputed magazines like *India Today, Trav Talk, Go Now* etc. Travel agents issue advertisements (without giving names of airlines) in newspapers.

Separate Business Class Fares : Austrian Airlines now flies you from Delhi to Vienna 4 times a week. Via the hub, Vienna International Airport, you have perfect connections to North America, Canada and more than *70* destinations in Western and Eastern Europe. And at Vienna Airport your ongoing flight will be only a few steps away.

Booking and Reservations : www.aua.com and at your travel agency.

Finally, brochures and catalogues are also printed (in four colours) to effect more sales.

Publicity: Travel agents, media persons and customers (medium and heavy uses) purchase the services of airlines. These may be given incentives to promote the services of the airline. PROs, executives, ticketing executives, marketing staff and sales staff of a travel agency do these jobs with great enthusiasm because they are in touch with existing and prospectus customers at all the times. Further, if the airline participates in air transport shows, tourism fairs, exhibitions and seminars, it displays its brand name, logo, life-size cut-outs etc to publicise its products and services. But it does not sell these at such occasions but only indulges in an awareness drive.

Sales Promotion: Free air packages for infants, discounted airfares for children of *2-10* years of age and special discounts for chartered flights are a part of this campaign. Passengers may be given free air bags, gifts or bottles of wine when they enter into the aircraft. They may be given discounts for their next air journeys (though the same airline). Frequent flyers are given heavy discounts. Passengers, who are supposed to take connecting flights, are not charged extra. Passengers can also move from the station of origin to the destination station and choose another station (in the sector) to come back to their station of origin. They can travel to that station of the sector travelled in by taxi, coach or rail. The airline can pick up the customer from a station that may be different firm the one, which is a part of the total itinerary. **Example:** DEL-BKK by Thai; BKK-SING by Thai; SING-KL by coach (Nice Travels); KL-BKK by a connected flight (MAS); BKK-DEL by Thai.

Personal Selling: These efforts are made by the staff of travel agencies Receptionists, sales girls at reception counters and booking executives undertake personal selling efforts on behalf of airlines that they represent. Tour operators and owners of resorts/hotels also indulge in personal selling exercises and promote those airlines with which, they are associated.

World-or-Mouth Promotion: Satisfied passengers tell their relatives and friends about the quality of services of airlines they had used for the purpose of domestic or international travel. So, those relatives and friends also prefer those very airlines. So much so, they also undertake those tours to domestic or foreign destinations that were undertaken by the actual customers.

Telemarketing Exercises: Travel agencies and tour operators appoint tele-marketers who sell airline packages and/or comprehensive tour packages to customers.

Distribution: Physical Based : It is synonymous with Place in the context of marketing management. Travel agencies, executives of tour operators, travel agents and producers of various services set up their offers at offices such places where tourists-to-be could approach them. Alternatively, these operators send their executives to homes/offices of these customers and deliver air tickets or documents related to packages, namely, passports with stamps of visas, transfer vouchers, tickets of night shows, tickets for entry to forts and museums etc.

Further, airlines are also able to provide excellent catering services to customers aboard the aircraft. Documents of customers are checked at airports by the airport authorities and customs officials. Customs duties are imposed on passengers who buy goods of values that are more than the value of free goods (i.e, those goods, which do not attract any customs duty). Hence, executives of travel agencies, tour operators, resorts, airport facilities and aircraft are a part of Place in the parlance of physical distribution efforts of airlines. The idea is to give two types of services to the customers core arid peripheral. At some times, the customer approaches the airline and at some others, the travel agency/ airline/tour operator/hotel owner/spot owner sends his representative or sales staff to the office or home of the customer.

Diverse Equipments : All the aircraft, cargo, handling equipment (like cranes, trolleys, container movers, lifts, maintenance equipment etc) aircraft maintenance machines, electrical utilities, mechanical utilities etc are a part of the technology that makes an airline operational.

Well-Trained Staff : The gargantuan tasks related to air travel cannot be executed without motivation and support of well-trained staff. Cabin crew, transporters to/from airport, truck operators, lift operators, maintenance staff, engineering staff etc are of part of the vital human resource that makes an airline transport system a success. Nowadays, there is emphasis on efficiency, performance and innovation and not just on a nine-to-five job. Airports have to be managed round-the-clock. International aircraft fly only after 10:00 pm from major airports. Airhostesses must remain on their toes at all the times. And our readers can understand fully well that managing an airborne vehicle carrying *300-400* passengers demands dexterity and perseverance of the caption of the aircraft. That is why, proper education and training in various streams of airline transport has become important nowadays.

Demands for Hotels : Under this concept, the basic idea is to convert light users (guests) of a hotel into medium users and medium users into heavy users. Competition is increasing in the hotel industry. So, poorly managed and: non-graded hotels may not survive in the times to come though they may remain favourites of the lower-end markets.

Demand for hotels increases if airline, cruise and coach bookings increase in terms of number of seats. If the tourist destination is a peaceful one (or located in a tourist country like Switzerland), these hotel bookings are regular. In some countries, demand is seasonal. Example: Hotel bookings in Shimla are full during the days of snowfall. During summer months, the hotels are booked to a large extent. But July, August and September are the lean months so far as hotel bookings are concerned. In southern India, snowfall is not the USP. But people visit popular tourist destinations throughout the year. In Goa, July and August are lean months. But December, January, February and May-June are the golden months.

Wars, ecological disasters and *force majeure'* affect hotel bookings in an adverse manner. Example; Hotel bookings in the gulf region were adversely affected in March-April, 2003 because of the Iraq--Us war. Tourists preferred not to visit the Gulf due to fierce fighting going on in Iraq. Although, the aircraft of the IA continued to fly to and from Kuwait city, yet people and tourists were generally not keen to move to that region due to fears related to this war.

Hotel's Product : The product of a hotel has a tangible component and an intangible component. The intangible component is equally important, just like the tangible one. Hotel professionals must design an overall package-that should make the customer realise that his money was well spent. Hotel rooms restaurant, cafe, shopping, entertainment and basic amenities like water, electricity, ventilation, air conditioning etc., are a part of the hotel product.

Product Mix Concepts of Hotel : The hotel has to define an adequate and guest-friendly product mix. The management of the hotel would have to define it according to the needs of guests, geographical setting of the hotel, category of the -hotel (like two-star, three-star etc) and policies of the government that are applicable to the hotel.

In order to define the product mix, the hotel owner must understand who his customers are. He has to study carefully their professional profiles, spending patterns and habits. Obviously, guests are not alike in terms of habits or stay patterns. But a few broad conclusions would 'certainly emerge. The hotel staff would allow only those customers to check into a five-star hotel who can afford the room rent of a five-star hotel; are effluent, car owners, businessmen, keen to indulge in dancing, drinking and activities of nightlife and spendthrift. They cannot be compared with the guests of a one-star hotel. So, the hotel would define a product mix that would suit the needs of his guests i.e, those guests who would fit into the category of the hotel. Competitors' hotel policies, facilities and products would also be important in this context. Another hotel in the vicinity of the hotel in question can pose a threat to the hotel. If the grades of both the hotels are the some, guests would compare the rooms, food, restaurant, peripheral services, hospitality - etc., of one hotel, with the other: Thus, if the hotel in question has at least one more hotel of the same class in its immediate vicinity, it should try to enhance or modify its product mix.

This would amount to giving more high-quality products and services at the same cost. Nowadays, hotels of three-star grade offer rooms and facilities that are better than those provided in four-star hotels. They understand that competitors are out to take away the vital market shares from them. So, they adopt this tactic to persuade the maximum number of guests to check in. But they cannot afford to call their ventures four-star hotels if they are three-star hotels. They only convince their guests that they are offering better services/products than those of their competitors. And their claims must actually be proved when the guests use their hotels.

Factors such as brand name (like the Oberoi Group), location of the hotel (like Bhikaji Cama Place), names of chefs (like Sanjiv Kapur), patronage of famous guests (like Michael Jackson in Hotel Oberoi Towers) and support of financial institutions (like the TFCI) also help the hotel owner define an exact product mix. This product mix has to be created in -a careful manner. It has also to be promoted with enthusiasm through various promotional tools and media. While defining the product mix of his hotel, the hotel owner should also take the travel agency or tour operator into confidence. These are the parts of marketing channels of tourism and know the demand sets of actual customers (who are buying tour packages and not mere accommodation and other services). Business tourists do not show interest in tourist spots; perhaps, they may have seen those and need not like to visit them again because they may too busy in their business transactions to undertake excursions. The hotel staff should not impose their tour packages on such business tourists. So, product mixes for business travellers and tourists would be different.

Finally, children women, old persons and teenagers have different requirements in the parlance of tourism. The hotel must be ready to cater to the precise needs of all of these customers. Example: The teenager son of a family may be keen to dance in the discotheque of the hotel but his parents may be keen to take rest in the room. The hotel staff should be quick enough to comprehend the needs of the teenager son and must not associate him with his parents while serving him.

Prices of Hotel Rooms : The price of a hotel room is associated with its grade or classification. Non-graded hotels do not have any pricing policies. But these are the ones that engage in bargaining with customers. Finally, the customer arrives at a decent price. In graded hotels, the question of bargaining on the price front does not arise. However, some hotels do offer price discounts, free bottles of wine, chocolates for children or free hotel-to city transfers. Local sight seeing is to be paid for if the guest has not planned it (with his travel agency).

The hotel product is also perishable. So, if a room remains vacant, the hotel loses money. This problem is being faced by graded hotels that cannot give discounts beyond certain limits. Guests also cannot force them to reduce prices. So, price reduction is voluntary according to the norms decided by the FHAII or other hotel organisations. Because of lean business cycles in 2002, the hotel owners of five-star hotels had to reduce the prices of luxury suites and economy suits by as much as *40 per cent*. Hence, sales had picked up during 2002. The government slaps heavy tax rates on five--star hotels. Seven-star hotels and intercontinental hotel are much more costlier than their five-tar cousins. Thus, the pricing policy of a hotel is controlled by the rules of the government. If they give discounts, they burn holes in their own pockets (as the government would take its share as taxes in any case).

Discounts differed by the hotel industry include:

(a) seasonal discounts (when the demand for rooms plummets);

(b) trade discounts (given to tour operators and travel agents so that they could earn their shares in the deals with tourists); and

(c) special discounts (special room rates for overnight stay or discounts on conference halls/banquet halls).

While fixing the room rent, the hotel management takes into account current rent rates; inflationary pressures, general economic state of the country, trends in currency change and competition.

While calculating the room rent, the net occupancy rate is calculated. It is multiplied with the costs of manufacturing the rooms of the hotel. Furnishing and air conditioning costs are also added to the figure. After adding all the costs, the profit percentage is decided. It can range from *10 per cent* to *20 per cent* of the basic cost. After profit has been added; taxes surcharges and other expenses (to be paid to the government) are added. We finally arrive at the room rent in the end. Guests can pay room rent by cheques, credit cards, cash or travellers cheques.

Pricing of food, liquor and beverages starts from the raw materials stage. All the raw materials are noted from the menu. The menu would tell us what materials to buy and the quantities of such raw materials. These costs are added. Then, processing, fuel, handling, refrigeration and human costs, which would be incurred to convert raw materials into completely cooked recipes, are calculated. Profit on the total basic cost varies from *5-10 per cent*. Then, sales tax is added; it is normally *7 per cent* of the final price. Over and above this price, the hotel changes a service tax of *10 per cent*. This tax is charged if the guest takes food and snacks in his room. The government may impose surcharge, taxes or levies on hotels. Such levies are added to the price calculated. Customers can clear their food and beverage bills by credit cards or travellers' cheques. They can also pay cash to clear the same.

CHAPTER–11

COMMODITIES AND PRODUCTS FOR HORTICULTURAL TOURISM

A commodity is a good for which there is demand, but which is supplied without qualitative differentiation across a market. A commodity has full or partial fungibility; that is, the market treats it as equivalent or nearly so no matter who produces it. Examples are petroleum and copper. The price of copper is universal, and fluctuates daily based on global supply and demand. Stereo systems, on the other hand, have many aspects of product differentiation, such as the brand, the user interface, the perceived quality etc. And, the more valuable a stereo is perceived to be, the more it will cost.

In contrast, one of the characteristics of a commodity good is that its price is determined as a function of its market as a whole. Well-established physical commodities have actively traded spot and derivative markets. Generally, these are basic resources and agricultural products such as iron ore, crude oil, coal, salt, sugar, coffee beans, soybeans, aluminium, copper, rice, wheat, gold, silver, palladium, and platinum. Soft commodities are goods that are grown, while hard commodities are the ones that are extracted through mining.

There is another important class of energy commodities which includes electricity, gas, coal and oil. Electricity has the particular characteristic that it is either impossible or uneconomical to store, hence, electricity must be consumed as soon as it is produced.

Commoditization (also called commodification) occurs as a goods or services market loses differentiation across its supply base, often by the diffusion of the intellectual capital necessary to acquire or produce it efficiently. As such, goods that formerly carried premium margins for market participants have become commodities, such as generic pharmaceuticals and silicon chips.

There is a spectrum of commodification, rather than a binary distinction of "commodity versus differentiable product". Few products have complete undifferentiability and hence fungibility; even electricity can be differentiated in the market based on its method of generation (e.g., fossil fuel, wind, solar). Many products' degree of commodification depends on the buyer's mentality and means. For example, milk, eggs, and notebook paper are considered by many customers as completely undifferentiable and fungible; lowest price is the only deciding factor in the purchasing choice. Other customers take into consideration other factors besides price, such as environmental sustainability and animal welfare. To these customers, distinctions such as organic-versus-not or cage-free-versus-not count toward differentiating brands of milk or eggs, and percentage of recycled content or forestry council certification count toward differentiating brands of notebook paper. Larger considerations can enter these equations, such as systemic socioeconomic unfairness (as poor people point out, "sure, it's easy to buy the expensive food when you've got plenty of money") and deception and authentication (e.g., a brand may greenwash its product and consumers lack practical ways to authenticate the claims).

As part of the drive towards sustainable agriculture there is a need systematically and holistically to assess the resource use and environmental burdens arising from alternative methods of production of agricultural and horticultural commodities. The technique of life cycle assessment (LCA) enables resource use and emissions arising from various agricultural and horticultural production options in England and Wales to be examined in detail.

The commodities examined in this project are: bread wheat, potatoes, oilseed rape, tomatoes, beef, pig meat, sheep meat, poultry meat, milk and eggs. The system boundary is the farm gate. All inputs into on-farm production are traced back to primary resources such as coal, crude oil and mined ore. All activities supporting farm production, such as feed production and processing, machinery and fertiliser manufacture, fertility building and cover crops are included. The system includes soil to a nominal depth of 0.3 m. All agricultural systems are defined so that they can continue for an infinite period time – thus weeds cannot be allowed to build up and nutrients in the soil cannot be depleted.

Abiotic resources used (ARU) are consolidated onto one scale based on relative scarcity. Individual emissions, such as carbon dioxide (CO_2), ammonia (NH_3) and nitrous oxide (N_2O), are quantified and aggregated into potentials for global warming (GWP), eutrophication (EP) and acidification (AP). Interactions between inputs, outputs and emissions are represented by functional relationships derived from process models wherever possible, so that as systems are modified they respond holistically to specific changes. For example, crop yields and nitrogen supply, dairy cow diet formulation and milk yield, and grass productivity, emissions, animal grazing and fertiliser applications are functionally related. Process simulation models are also used to derive the long term outcomes of nitrate leaching, soil, crop type and nitrogen supply.

Main findings:

1. Nitrous oxide is the single largest contributor to global warming potential (GWP) for most commodities, exceeding 80% in some cases. There is the least understanding about the reliable quantification of this emission.
2. Organic field crops and animal products generally consume less primary energy than non-organic counterparts owing to the use of legumes to fix N rather than fossil energy to make synthetic fertilisers. Poultry meat and eggs are exceptions, resulting from the very high efficiency of feed conversion in the non-organic sector.
3. There is much greater variation in the relative burdens of GWP, acidification potential (AP) and eutrophication potential (EP) between organic and non-organic field-based commodities than there is in their energy use.
4. Yields (t/ha) are lower for organic than for conventional production such that for a given amount of output more land is always required for organic production (65% to 200% extra).
5. All arable crops incur smaller burdens per tonne than meats, but all commodities have different nutritional properties and energy requirements beyond the farm, so care must be taken in comparisons.
6. Ruminant meats incur more burdens than pig or poultry meats, but ruminants can derive nutrition from land that is unsuitable for the arable crops required by pigs and poultry.
7. Heating and lighting dominate the burdens of long-season tomato production; adopting combined heat and power (CHP) technology could reduce the primary energy consumption by about 70%.

8. Non-organic, loose classic tomatoes incur the least burdens per tonne of produce (in long-season production) and they increase progressively towards organic, on-the-vine specialist types.

The main burdens of commodity production are shown below for England and Wales. As the market share for organic production is relatively small, these values essentially are for conventional non-organic production. The numbers may differ slightly from those in the published report as improvements have been made in the model since initial publication.

FICCI for FDI in Retail to Tame Food Inflation

At a time when the government and common man both is grappling with double-digit food inflation, the Federation of Indian Chambers of Commerce and Industry (FICCI) has come out with a 5-point package of measures that includes according accord special status to perishables and horticulture commodities and de-listing of horticulture commodities from the schedule-I containing notified commodities in APMR Acts of all states.

The Chamber has suggested that FDI in retail should be permitted with the stipulation that the organised retail chains would work closely with farmers in imparting better know-how and providing inputs to improve the productivity and directly sourcing from farmers.

Food inflation has been in double digits for more than a year, primarily due to severe pressure from fruits and vegetables, eggs, meat and marine products. "The government should look at addressing the structural issues related to APMC Act in order to ensure that food inflation is effectively controlled," the chamber said.

According to FICCI, the present onion crisis is no doubt a direct consequence of supply side constraints; the situation is further aggravated by the monopoly of traders in APMCs created by the provisions of the APMR Act.

Most of the APMCs limit the number of licenses issued in a particular market, thereby restricting and eliminating competition required for efficient market functioning. As a result, in situations of limited supply of a particular commodity, the prices get artificially inflated due to limited number of colluded traders.

In this context, FICCI has argued that there is an urgent need to accord a special status to perishables and horticulture commodities. The horticulture commodities should be de-listed from the schedule-I containing notified commodities in APMR Acts of all states. By doing so, it would mean that anyone can buy or sell only perishable commodities anywhere in the country. This would also mean that zone of influence of perishables would be beyond states resulting in better prices for farmers and stabilised prices for consumers. The long chain of intermediaries and inefficient price discovery mechanism are the reasons for high price mark-ups between farmers and consumers. Therefore, farmers should be encouraged to form producer associations/ farmer co-operatives and aggregate the produce, which could be directly sold on electronic spot exchanges or to retailers at consumption centers, FICCI said.

Further, all the markets should be e-linked by introducing electronic auctions or electronic spot exchange counters for transparent price discovery. This would lead to improved efficiency and better price discovery for both the farmers and consumers, the chamber said.

It also suggested that the government should look at encouraging truck operators to operate fleet of transport carriers with special green permits, which would permit them to swiftly move across the border with minimal inspections.

Exempt Horticulture from APMC Act

With the spectre of high food inflation haunting the economy, the Confederation of Indian Industry's National

Council on Agriculture has sought structural changes to augment growth in the farm sector.

In an interview with Business Line, Mr Rakesh Bharti Mittal, Chairman, CII National Council on Agriculture, and Vice-Chairman and Managing Director, Bharti Enterprise Ltd, outlines some corrective measures such as opening up FDI in multi-brand retail and also exempting horticulture produce from the APMC Act.

With food inflation peaking at 19.9 per cent, he says farm-to-fork mechanism can be best achieved when the Government enters into a "mission mode", both at national and State level.

CII has been saying that there is a deeper structural problem in the way we manage our food security? What are the issues dogging the sector?

We strongly believe that the agriculture sector in India has to get into a mission mode both at national and at the state level. Anything that gets into a mission gets monitored and supervised. The Ministry of Agriculture must look at it seriously to avoid future food security issues. If timely interventions are made, it can help farmers at one end of the spectrum. We have come out with various recommendations where we have said that the Government should come out with input stamps, which means all subsidies must be through input stamps wherein the farmers must be at liberty to use subsidy for fertiliser, micro-irrigation, seeds or pesticides. While fertiliser subsidy may be indirect subsidy, this may go directly to the farmer. Input tax will give farmers flexibility.

You have also made some recommendations regarding land? What exactly are they?

Yes. We have also made recommendations on lease of agricultural land. Today it is regulated by an Act. It is 17-22 hectares in certain States. Small and medium farmers have about 1-2 acres and you can't use machinery and technology on such small holdings. So farm productivity is getting saturated. Unless interventions are made at a large scale, small and medium farmers will not benefit.

Therefore we are saying that if lease of agri-land is undertaken then small and medium farmers can aggregate land and private sector can come in.

Two suggestions we have made is that all State Governments must allow it (lease) and it should be permitted in long tenures, only then private companies will bring in technologies. Also government through legislation should say that the ownership will not change and leases will not have any tenancy rights, which means land will remain with the owners. That is the only way to take agriculture to the next level. Absentee farmers are not giving their land and that is putting pressure on agriculture.

The third area we have talked about is research and extension. Very few initiatives have happened after the Green Revolution. That is where private sector needs to come into play.

Our own company Fieldfresh works with 4,000 farmers and provides extension services. In this case, we have recommended that average weighted deduction of 200 per cent should be allowed in the research and extension services. Statutes and regulation need to be changed, otherwise agriculture will continue to struggle.

Wastage of perishable goods has been a long-standing concern? How can it be reduced to ensure that both famers and consumers get the best price?

We have been talking about the APMC Act in the last 7-8 years. Seventeen States have given a thumbs-up but it is not being implemented in letter and spirit. They have gone about arbitrarily making changes. The pressure of middlemen is also preventing State Governments from going ahead in full steam.

Therefore, we are saying exempt horticulture from APMC Act.

Farmers should be given the freedom to sell their produce directly to a food processing company, a consolidator or a retailer. Time will be shortened. Today you need licence to buy agri products. Why should there be licence for agri product? This will take care of food inflation.

You have been strongly advocating FDI in multi brand retail. How will this change the retail canvass?

For long we have said that opening up of the retail sector is beneficial for the industry as investments in organised retail will scale up the entire supply chain and ensure good prices to farmers as well as consumers. Today fresh produce moves at an ambient temperature, which leads to tremendous wastages. Opening up the sector will create infrastructure.

What are the recommendations which you would like to see implemented in the near term?

In the short term, we are seeking lowering of import duty, especially on fruit and vegetables, and imports. Looking at the rising prices of fruit and vegetables, the Government should react fast on lowering the existing tariffs (hovering around 30-50 per cent) and allow import of these commodities. The Government should incentivise private sector (both domestic and foreign), cooperatives and NGOs to come up with business models that directly link the growers with processors and retailers.

COMMODITIES BUZZ: INDIA'S HORTICULTURE CROPS

The Horticulture crops output has grown by an impressive 7% per year for the last five years and has potential to boost overall agriculture growth in the country, according to a latest press release from the Ministry of Agriculture. Horticulture has seen significant jump in area, production and export with help from the National Horticulture Mission in the last five years.

The interventions under the Mission have helped in increasing the production of horticultural commodities from 166.9 million tonnes in 2004-05 to 226.9 million tonnes by 2009-10, registering a growth rate of about seven percent per year. There has been consistent increase in the exports of horticultural produce, which has reached the level of Rs. 13,423.76 crore during 2009-10.

In the last five years, an area of 16.57 lakh hectares has been brought under horticultural crops since the launch of the mission. Organic farming has also been taken up in 1.37 lakh ha.

Under post harvest management, 1091 pack houses, 285 cold storage units, 4 controlled Atmosphere (CA) stores, 16 refrigerated vans and 264 mobile/ primary processing units have been set up. Moreover, 172 markets, including 9 wholesale markets, have been established for facilitating marketing of horticulture produce.

Rs. 8809 crore has been earmarked for the Mission during the Eleventh Plan, out of which Rs. 2728 has been released till 2009-10. A provision of Rs. 986 crore has been earmarked for the current year (2010-11) against which an amount of Rs. 779.20 crore has been released so far.

Kenya

Kenya's economy is market-based, with a few state-owned infrastructure enterprises, and maintains a liberalized external trade system. The country is generally perceived as Eastern and central Africa's hub for Financial, Communication and Transportation services. As at May 2010, economic prospects are positive with 4-5% GDP growth expected, largely because of expansions in tourism, telecommunications, transport, construction and a recovery in agriculture. These improvements are supported by a large pool of English speaking professional workers. There is a high level of computer literacy, especially among the youth. The government, generally perceived as investment friendly, has enacted several regulatory reforms to simplify both foreign and local investment. An increasingly significant portion of Kenya's foreign inflows is from remittances by non-resident Kenyans who work in the US, Middle East, Europe and Asia. Compared to its neighbors, Kenya has a well developed social and physical infrastructure. It is considered the main alternative location to South Africa, for major corporations seeking entry into the African continent.

Kenya's services sector, which contributes about 63 percent of GDP, is dominated by tourism. The tourism sector has exhibited steady growth in most years since independence and by the late 1980s had become the country's principal source of foreign exchange. In the late 1990s, tourism relinquished this position to tea exports, because of a terrorism-related downturn. The downturn followed the 1998 bombing of the U.S Embassy in Nairobi and later negative travel advisories from Western governments. Tourists, the largest number from Germany and the United Kingdom, are attracted mainly to the coastal beaches and the game reserves, notably, the expansive Tsavo National Park (20,808 square kilometers) in the southeast. The government and tourist industry organizations have taken steps to address the security problem and to reverse negative publicity. Such steps include establishing a tourist police and launching marketing campaigns in key tourist origin markets. Tourism has seen a substantial revival over the past several years and is the major contributor to the pick-up in the country's economic growth.

Tourism is now Kenya's largest foreign exchange earning sector, followed by flowers, tea, and coffee. In 2006 tourism generated US$803 million, up from US$699 million the previous year.

Products for Horticulture Tourism

We are reputed exporters and suppliers of fresh flower, floral gifts / chocolates, dry materials & floral accessories and other agriculture products. Beside these, we are also into various other activities like agriculture, horticulture, floriculture and tissue culture. Along with that, we provide consultancy services in the field of agriculture & horticulture like flower farming services, flower cultivation services, floral decorations services and floral delivery services. Our flower farming services, flower cultivation services and floral decorations services are rendered to various clients spread across the globe. Some of our services and products are enlisted below :

Floriculture (Flower Farming)— We are specialized in floriculture or flower farming which is quite popular in every country. Now a day's different variety of flowers are extensively used for decoration and gifting purpose. We are engaged in cultivating a wide variety of flowers using advanced scientific techniques of farming. The entire process of cultivation, irrigation, plantation of vegetation is effectively carried out by our trained workmen to maintain the productivity. Along with that, we are also a leading exporter, retailer and whole seller of fresh cut flowers, filers and foliages. One of our associate company Trimurthy Enterprises offers floral foams, fresh floral foams, bricks, dry material and fresh floral accessories in bulk quantity.

Floral Services—Cater to the requirements of retail flower arrangements, flower bouquets, pausseys etc. Organise floral decorations for all occasions & events, delivery and supply of floral gifts. Also handle landscaping & landscape design, garden execution & maintenance, supply of flowering and ornamental pot plant.

Tissue Culture Plants, Pot Plants & Ornaments— We use culture medium for tissue culture plant, which is a technique of growing different species of plants in large scale. Actively growing shoot tips of tissue culture plants are being cultured using organic (macronutrients, micronutrients, & vitamins) and inorganic salts, energy source (sucrose or table sugar), growth regulators and agar. These proliferated shoots are being rooted in special medium called peat-perlite medium to make plantlets (miniature plants). Our bulk tissue culture plants like gypsophilias, anthuriums, limoniums, orchids, cordilines, caladiums, spathyphyllums and others are being stored in our well built nursery and exported to clients spread across the globe.

Horticulture & Cultivation Services—We are engaged in horticulture services where we try to cultivate different species of fruits and vegetables on large scale. Our process is carried out after conducting rigorous research work. We have highly qualified horticulturist who looks after the entire process to ensure top notch quality fruits and vegetables. The chemicals which we use in the process are harmless and help in the growth of the various plants.

Seed Production—We are specialized in hybrid Seed Production of different vegetables and flowers. These hybrid seeds are produce through open pollinated method through standardized culture and storage practice. We use high quality chemicals to protect the vegetable seed and flower seed from insects, pests.

Agriculture & Horticulture Consultancy—We are leading agri-horti consultants; our horticulture consultancy, agriculture consultancy and agricultural horticultural consultants ensures quality output and timely delivery. Our methodology is counted among best practices in the industry. We give information on conventional & current happenings of agriculture sector. Our horticulture consultancy, agriculture consultancy and agricultural horticultural consultants provide guidance on usage of new technology, latest industrial up gradation to various clients.

Branding & Marketing for Domestic & Export Markets—We do effective branding & marketing of our agriculture products locally as well as globally. Our sales and marketing executives are well knowledgeable in branding and marketing of our agriculture product. Proper brand name is given to the products to create an identity among our diversified clients. Due to our effective branding process, we are able to market our product smoothly. We are offering agricultural produce harvesting, fruit ripening, agricultural produce marketing and fruit ripening process.

Eco-tourism—Eco tourism centre – To undertake activities like perma culture; organize for home stays, to organize field visits as a part of educational tour and training programmes in organic cultivation, conservation of eco-system, apiculture, medicinal & aromatic plants etc for schools & colleges.

Organic Farming— Adhere to organic farming and organic practices to replace the conventional supplies and produce of vegetables & fruits with only organic products. To organize for planting material, seeds, certified organic bio-fertilizers & bio-pesticides, to establish a seed bank for storing organic seeds, setup facility for preparation of bio pesticides and bio fertilizers. Start an organic research institute to formulate strategies and develop know how for pest & disease control, organic cultural practices, plant nutritional aspects, integrated pest management and related techniques for precision agriculture. Conduct training programmes for farming community & educational institutions.

CHAPTER–12

HORTICULTURAL TOURISM: RISK & LIABILITY

A liability risk involves the threat of the company or individual having to bear the consequences of damage or of breaching standards due to operations, a product, an act or neglect. A liability risk survey involves the analysis, through interviews and review of documents, of the company's key liability risks. The liability risk survey can cover all of the company's liability risks or only those of agreed sectors. The tool used is the If Liability Navigator.

General Liability risk refers to the risk of the company's operations causing damage to the company's employees, contractual parties or third parties.

Product Liability risk refers to the risk of a product launched by the company causing damage to a person or to other property.

Contractual risk refers to the risk of contracts not being fulfilled properly or within the agreed time limit, which can result in losses and other consequences for the company.

The survey may also focus on the liability of the service provider, environmental liability, liability for the breach of an intangible right and Directors' and Officers' liability.

AGRITOURISM RISKS & LIABILITIES

Farmers wanting to get into the agritourism industry can better understand the risks and potential liability they will face by attending a workshop being held next month in conjunction with the Indiana Horticultural Congress and Trade Show.

The workshop will be on Jan. 18 at the Wyndham Hotel, 2544 Executive Drive, in Indianapolis near the old airport terminal.

Participants will learn about risks and liability associated with such agritourism activities and operations such as hayrides, workshops, seasonal festivals, petting zoos, bed-and-breakfast inns and wineries.

"The list of entertaining and educational opportunities right here in Indiana seems almost limitless," said Roy Ballard, a Purdue Extension agriculture and natural resources educator in Hancock County and a workshop organizer. "But an issue that farmers must consider before entering into an agritourism venture or expanding an existing operation is how to manage risk and limit liability when inviting the public onto a working farm."

One session will feature a panel of producers who will discuss how they manage risk as part of their business planning. They are Amy Kelsay of Kelsay Farms, Whiteland; Greg Hochstedler of Boondocks Farm, Knightstown; and Tom Dull of Dull's Tree Farm, Thorntown.

There also will be a roundtable discussion for those who have an agritourism venue or are considering the possibility and want to share experiences, opportunities and trends in the industry.

Featured speakers and titles of their presentations include:

- Phil Lehmkuhler, Indiana state director of USDA Rural Development, "The State of Rural Indiana and the Role of Agritourism in its Future."

- Shannon Mirus, staff attorney for the National Agricultural Law Center, University of Arkansas, "Anticipating and Managing Risk and Liability in Your Agritourism Venture" and "What is Limited Liability for Agritourism and How Are Other States Employing It?"
- Debbie Trocha, director of the Indiana Cooperative Development Center, "An Indiana Direct-to-Consumer Association: How Can it Benefit Your Operation?"

Employer Liability Costs

Britain's small businesses could face crippling rises in employer liability insurance premiums due to new regulations, warns Bibby Financial Services - the largest specialist provider of business cash flow solutions.

Changes to the Health and Social Care Act, which came in to effect last month, now give the NHS the power to recoup treatment costs from firms that have been proved negligent in the case of employee accidents in the workplace.

Andrew Dixon of Bibby Financial Services, said: "As the UK moves towards a 'compensation culture' the necessity for businesses to have adequate liability cover in place is more important than ever. However, for many businesses the rise in insurance premiums is simply a cost they cannot absorb. Almost half (46%) of UK business owners and managers claim they cannot afford an increase in liability premiums, with over two thirds (67%) concerned that further hikes will force them to close their doors.*

"The good news for employers is that insurers are willing to work with the business community to minimise additional costs, by reflecting responsible health and safety practices in their rates. Businesses that wish to reduce their liability cover costs should heed the advice of the insurance industry and ensure they have cohesive health and safety policies in place."

In order to help business owners and managers tackle the often complex area of health and safety in the workplace, Bibby Financial Services has developed the following tips:

- Get registered - if you have at least one employee you must register with the appropriate body. If you have employees in an office or shop, you need to register with your local council. If you have a factory, you must register with the Health and Safety Executive.
- Assess the risk - whether you are an employer or work alone, you are legally required to assess the risks in your workplace. Carrying out a risk assessment is the first step in minimising the cost of health and safety by ensuring that the correct preventative measures are in place.
- Review and revise - review your risk assessment on an annual basis and always amend your assessment when circumstances change (e.g. when you buy a new piece of equipment). Remember to record the outcome of your risk assessment and any corrective action taken.
- Put it in writing - if you employ more than five people, you must have a written health and safety policy and make sure that it is brought to the attention of all your employees. The policy should include: your general approach to safety, any people you appoint to look after health and safety matters and any specific health and safety procedures and emergency instructions you have in place
- Training matters - ensure that you provide appropriate health and safety training for all employees. Include health and safety training as part of an employees induction and always monitor their behaviour to ensure that training is effective and that the procedures are being followed.

- Look after your staff - as an employer, you have a legal obligation to provide enough clean, working toilets, drinking water, clean working areas, comfortable temperatures, adequate lighting, space, ventilation and an appropriate rest area
- In case of an accident - you must have suitable first aid facilities and under the Reporting of Injuries, Diseases and Dangerous Occurrences Regulations (RIDDOR) you are required to report serious injuries, diseases and dangerous incidents. All businesses must have an accident book that records the date and details of each accident, including the name of the injured person and what action was taken.
- If in any doubt, ask - your local authority, the Health and Safety Executive (HSE) or your local Chamber of Commerce or Business Link will be able to point you in the right direction for further information. Independent health and safety consultants can also provide useful advice.

While providing a safe and healthy working environment is a priority for many businesses, in reality, the majority find the day-to-day reality of risk assessments and compliance time consuming and a distraction from their core business activity.

Andrew Dixon added: "In an increasingly litigious society, it's in every business' best interest to ensure they come up to scratch when it comes to health and safety matters. Not only can the personal consequences be devastating if a staff member or customer is injured, but business output can be lost, machinery damaged and insurance costs increased. With numerous low-cost outsourcing options now available, small business owners and managers no longer have to tackle complex health and safety issues alone.

"The solution for many owners and managers is to outsource their health and safety requirements, in the same way they outsource other non-core functions of the business.

CREDIT RISK IN LIABILITY MEASUREMENT

The issue is relevant to a number of the IASB's projects - in particular in the accounting for financial instruments, insurance, fair value measurement and provisions, contingent liabilities and contingent assets.

The project team has completed analysing the responses received on the IASB's invitation to comment. The staff paper referred to in the invitation to comment outlines the three most often-cited arguments in favour of including credit risk in current measurement of liabilities and the three most often-cited arguments against. The comment period for the paper closed 1 September 2009. View the comment letters received **here**.

The IASB started discussing the responses to the discussion paper in its September 2009 board meeting and completed its discussions in October 2009. At its October meeting the Board decided to stop work on credit risk as a free-standing work stream and agreed not to reach a general conclusion on credit risk at this time. It will incorporate the topic in the conceptual framework measurement project. Additionally the Board decided not to change the role of credit/performance risk in the definition of fair value result of the responses to this DP. Finally the Board decided to consider the application of the fair value definition in every project involving measurements that would otherwise be at fair value and consider the question of credit risk in every project involving a current measurement of liabilities that is not fair value.

The Board is discussing credit risk in liability measurement in the project to replace IAS 39 and further information can be found **here**.

CHAPTER–13

HORTICULTURAL TOURISM: SUCCESSES AND CHALLENGES

Horticultural crop production creates jobs. On average it provides twice the amount of employment per hectare of production compared to cereal crop production (Ali et al., 2002). The move from cereal production towards high-value horticulture crops is an important contributor to employment opportunities in developing countries (Joshi et al., 2003). The horticultural commodity chain is also longer and more complex than the cereal crop one and as a result job opportunities are more abundant (Temple, 2001).

Women have the most to benefit from the increasing importance of horticulture in rural economies. Women, in general, play a much more significant role in horticultural crop production compared to starchy staple crops. For example in Bangladesh, women account for 48% of all labor in vegetable production compared to only 11-20% for cereal production (Rahman, 2000). Similar findings were made in Latin America and Africa (Weinberger and Lumpkin, 2005). Throughout the developing countries of Africa, women play a dominant role in the production of horticultural crops and cultivate more than half of the total smallholdings.

Besides creating jobs on the farm, the horticultural sector also generates off-farm employment, especially for women. This is the case for export and value-added processing industries, which are important sectors of the economies of Latin America and Africa. In Mexico, for example, 80-90% of people engaged in packing operations are women, and even higher percentages of women workers are involved in fresh produce field operations. Evidence from Africa reflects a similar trend: women comprise 91 % of horticultural employees in Zimbabwe (Dolan and Sorby, 2003). Since horticultural production is very labor-intensive, landless laborers also benefit from the new employment opportunities created by horticultural crop production. These jobs usually provide more income than jobs obtained by the laborers in most other sectors (Weinberger and Genova, 2005; Weinberger and Lumpkin, 2005).

IMPROVED FOOD SECURITY AND NUTRITION

All of the hungry and many of the overweight are afflicted with micronutrient deficiency (lack of vitamins and minerals). Over two billion people, the vast majority of whom are women and children, suffer from micronutrient deficiencies (UN/SCN, 2004; Gardner and Halwell, 2000). Horticultural crops can play a vital role in solving this global micronutrient crisis. Vegetables and fruits are the most sustainable and affordable sources of micronutrients in diets (UN, 2004).

Healthy diets improve the learning capacity of children and the productivity of workers (Weinberger, 2004). In contrast, micronutrient-deficient diets lead to reduced mental and physical development, poor performance in school, loss of productivity in the workplace, and the likelihood of poverty in future generations (Haddad et al., 2002).

Vitamin A deficiency alone weakens the immune system of 40% of children in developing countries (UN, 2004). This deficiency increases a child's risk of severe illness and death from infectious diseases, which are the leading causes of death in developing countries. Vitamin A deficiency contributes to higher rates of anemia as well as morbidity from common childhood infections such as respiratory and diarrheal diseases (Sommer and West, 1996), measles (West, 2000) and malaria (Shankar et al., 1999). Deficiencies of vitamin A and other micronutrients may increase the likelihood of HIV/AIDS transmission from mother to child and hasten the progression of the disease in infected persons (Fawzi et al., 2002; Semba et al., 1994).

Iron deficiency affects at least 2 billion, and perhaps up to 3.5 billion people. Shortage of iron in the diet causes reduced productivity, which results in economic losses of billions of dollars globally (Weinberger, 2004; UN, 2004). These losses are so substantial that economists at the Copenhagen Consensus in 2004 agreed that relieving iron and other micronutrient deficiencies should be the second highest priority in world development initiatives, second only to relieving the HIV/AIDS crisis (Economist, 2004).

Although essential in diets, not enough vegetables and fruits are available, especially to poor families in developing countries. Rates of production of vegetables and fruits cannot satisfy consumer demand and these micronutrient-rich food sources are often too expensive for the poor. Production of vegetables and fruits unfortunately is often accompanied by misuse and abuse of pesticides with their negative effects on human health and potential impact on the environment. In the least developed countries, the consumption of fruits and vegetables is declining (FAO 2004b). Steps must be taken to reverse this trend through provision of a range of safe, affordable and nutritious vegetables.

HORTICULTURAL EXPORTS SUCCESS

Kenyan horticultural exports are often cited as a success story in African agriculture. Fruit and vegetable exports from

Côte 'Ivoire have received less attention, but the export value is similar to that of Kenya. This paper focuses on three questions. First, do the horticultural sectors of Kenya and Côte d'Ivoire constitute valid success stories? Second, what factors have contributed to the success (or lack thereof)? And third, to what degree can the success be replicated in other African countries?

The paper finds that Kenyan horticultural exports are indeed a success story: horticulture has become the third largest earner of foreign exchange, more than half the exports are produced by smallholders, and smallholders gain from producing for the export market. At the same time, the total number of smallholders producing for export is relatively small, and trends in European retailing may shift the advantage to larger producers. Côte d'Ivoire is not as clearly a success story because the most of the exports are produced on large industrial estates and because growth has been uneven. Ivorian exports rely on preferential access to European markets relative to Latin American exporters, raising doubts about sustainability.

Factors in the growth and success of horticultural exports include a realistic exchange rate, stable policies, a good investment climate, competitive international transport connections, institutional, and social links with markets in Europe, and continual experimentation with the market institutions to link farmers and exporters. Smallholder participation is encouraged by farmer training and extension schemes, investment in small-scale irrigation, and assistance in establishing links with exporters. Many of the lessons of Kenyan horticulture can be applied elsewhere in Africa. Indeed, Kenya faces increasing competition from neighboring countries trying to replicate its success. At the same time, market institutions take time to develop, and demand constraints probably prevent other African countries from achieving the same level of success as Kenya.

CASE STUDY

International Gardening and Horticulture Exposition to be Held in Taipei

Entering its final one-year countdown, Hau vowed that the expo, which will give Taipei City a face-lift by upgrading its software and hardware facilities, will once again take the capital city to the international limelight and make its citizens proud.

Scheduled to be held for the first time in Taiwan from Nov. 6, 2010 to April 25, 2011, the Taipei Int'l Flora Expo is the first category A2B1 world exposition for Taiwan to host under the authorization of the Netherlands-based International Association of Horticultural Producers (AIPH). Taipei is the seventh city in Asia to host international players in the horticulture industry.

Flora Expo: Taipei's new interaction with the world

Managing to squeeze time out of his busy schedule, Hau made an inspection tour to major exhibitions halls of the expo Thursday. Hau stood in front of the EXPO Hall and mapped out his vision, saying that the main objective of the expo is to "let the world see Taipei, and let Taipei embrace the world."

Noting that the test operation of the expo will kick off in September 2010, Hau estimated that the 171-day event will attract over 6 million visitors from home and abroad, and with a total investment of NT$3.529 billion, the expo will create a minimum economic benefit of NT$11.7 billion (US$360 million) — roughly 1.5 to 3 times the investment amount based on statistics of previous events held worldwide.

Business or industries such as horticulture, tourism and travel, restaurants and bio-technology are also expected to benefit, which Hau said would be a great boost in revitalizing Taiwan's economy.

Hau noted that Taiwan has always enjoyed a great reputation for and taken pride in its advancement in horticulture and bio-technology, with world-acclaimed orchid productions and celebrated rice and fruit growing technologies.

Moreover, Taipei is a modern city rich in cultural and natural resources, Hau said, citing as examples the city's annual output value of US$50 billion in the high-tech industry; the more than 640,000 pieces of historic and cultural treasures housed in the National Palace Museum, as well as hot spring sites and volcanic geography in Yangmingshan National Park.

"All of these features will be showcased in the expo not only to increase Taipei's international profile but also to promote global understanding of Taiwan," Hau said.

Support ofTaipei Citizens key to The success

Hau admitted that there were obstacles and frustrations over the past two years in preparing for the expo because unlike previous flora expos held in Europe, Japan or China, the 2010 Taipei expo will be the first to be held in city center.

High population density, frequent industrial and commercial activities, and great transportation volume made it extremely difficult to find permanent sites for constructing the pavilions, Hau said.

Minimizing the impacts on traffic and how to move the temporary pavilions for future use, all posed great challenges to the city government, according to Hau, adding that "reduce, reuse and recycle" are the key concepts when designing the pavilions.

"I, however, have good faith in our citizens. While the city government is doing all it can to accomplish the arduous task, I believe that everybody will offer his or her greatest support to help us market Taipei and create a first-class international image," Hau said.

When 2010 Taipei Int'l Expo meets ROC Centennial anniversary

With world-class exhibition scale, content and participants, Hau said the Taipei flora expo will be of special meaning given the fact that the Republic of China will also be celebrating its centennial birthday in 2011, as many other countries did when they hosted the event, such as Italy, Canada and Australia.

Featuring the theme of "Flower, River, New Horizon," the Taipei Expo will include 14 unique exhibition pavilions, eight of which are remodeled from existing buildings while the rest are new constructions, to bring about the characteristics of "flora and horticulture," "culture and arts," "environmental ecology" and "pioneering technology."

Hau said there is no better stage than the 2010 Taipei expo for Taiwan to showcase its strength in horticulture and flora industry, as the event is the most prestigious professional horticultural exposition in the world.

Five pavilions are dedicated for this purpose, including the EXPO Dome and Pavilion of Culture in the Yuanshan Park Area, and Pavilion of Future, Pavilion of Life and Palace of Floral Teas in Xinsheng Park Area, he added.

Environmental ecology also plays a significant role in the expo, Hau said, not only because environmental protection is a common responsibility of human beings, but also because of the fact that global warming has become an international hot issue.

Concepts of ecological conservation and resources recycling were embodied in the design of the EXPO Theater, a three-dimensional theater which will show a film titled "Face the Reality of the Earth" to increase awareness of ecological crisis in Taiwan, he added.

In addition, five pavilions are designed to demonstrate Taiwan's diversified cultures and arts, including Celebrity's House, Pavilion of New Fashion, Pavilion of Aroma of

Flowers and the EXPO Hall, while Pavilion of Future, Pavilion of Dreams and Pavilion of Life will showcase Taiwan's excellent pioneering technologies.

Taipei Expo Expected to Create Immense Business Opportunities

Taipei city government's Department of Economic Development estimates that the 2010 Taipei flora expo is expected to attract six million visitors, including 300,000 from abroad. It is also expected to generate NT$11.7 billion in economic benefits and create 63,000 jobs.

Promising to purchase more than 40 million flowers and plants for the exposition by local floriculture industry and producers, Hau said the event also provides a great opportunity to display Taiwan's native flower and plant species on the international stage and show the world Taiwan's vitality.

According to Hau, the flora expo will not only bring economic benefits to the floriculture producers, but also help promote growth in industries such as green architecture, landscaping, and exhibition and convention.

Public Participation and International Propaganda

Entering the final year of preparation, how to increase the public's participation and enthusiasm for the event and how to promote international propaganda are two major challenges for the Taipei city government, according to Hau.

In response to the challenges, his team will establish more "city gardens" and install large green sculptures at major railway stations to trumpet up public interests in the event, Hau said.

Moreover, the mayor said the city government will model its successful experience in hosting the Deaflympics to recruit volunteers from the private sector, such as schools, companies and non-governmental organizations, so as to show foreign visitors the warmth of Taiwanese people.

ENTENTE FLORALE

After its great success in winning The Small Coastal Resort Award in the recent Royal Horticultural Society's Britain in Bloom competition, St. Brelade has been honoured by The European Association for Flowers and Landscape with the request to represent The United Kingdom in their Annual Competition, among 12 European Countries, which have entered their best Towns and Villages for assessment by a Panel of Judges appointed by each entering Country. The competition was initiated in 1975 and St. Brelade has been put forward by The Royal Horticultural Society with the aim to achieve Gold or Silver Awards under the Entente Florale revised rules introduced in 1996.

The European entries are supported by Ministries, Departments of Agriculture, Tourism, horticulture bodies and associations in each Country and by companies with Corporate, Social Responsibility principles. The prestigious Awards bring international publicity and encourage village and town life and the development of tourism to the benefit of the larger communities around them.

The European Association for Flowers and Landscape describes its aims:

- Our Association is an international non-profit association, and its overall aims are social and cultural development to enhance Horticulture, Tourism and Environment.
- For realizing these aims we encourage actions that foster a better quality of life for urban dwellers.
- The Association organizes an international competition known as 'Entente Florale Europe', in order to promote a greener and more pleasant environment in European towns and villages and to facilitate international contacts among the participants, based on reference towns and villages network.

- Through this annual competition, public authorities, private bodies and individuals are encouraged to cooperate in beautifying their towns and villages thereby improving the quality of life for both inhabitants and visitors, by the planting of flowers and shrubs, by the development and maintenance of green spaces and parks and by generally fostering development which is ecologically and environmentally sensitive.

The Aim of the Competition

The overall aim of the competition is the improvement of the quality of life for local urban and village communities. To this end the competition fosters:

- the greening of towns and villages
- flowers, shrubs, green spaces, parks
- development which is environmentally and ecologically sensitive
- educational and communication initiatives which promote environmental awareness.

St. Brelade is specifically invited as the Village to represent The United Kingdom in 2010.

This would be the first entry from The States of Jersey for the European Entente Florale, since the original inception of the competition in 1975. Whether Gold or Silver is awarded to Villages and Towns which enter these competitions, there are Marketing and Promotion opportunities for the communities around the Towns, and Villages receiving these awards and for the organizations which support the entry with sponsorship.

The cost of the UK entry includes a cost/fee paid through the Royal Horticultural Society to the Entente Florale of 2,100 Euros, which is administered by the RHS and allocated 2/3rd to the Town and 1/3rd to the Village Entry. The total cost reported by the village of Forres from their Gold Award entry to the 2009 Competition was £5,634 including presentations, publications and accommodation and entertainment of the Judges. Towns and some villages in Europe make a major event of the judges' attendance in their communities, with pageants and musical events, but that is not intended to be, nor is it a consideration in the process of awarding points under the many categories of floral, environmental, and educational achievement which form their judgment. We can assume a total cost to St. Brelade of around £6,000. The visiting UK Judge informed the meeting, 30.11.09, that sum needed would be less than £10,000. However, as this project would bring a significant increase in tourists generally, it is thought that a donation from the States Tourism Department would be fitting. This entry needs to be covered by grants and by underwriting by February 2010.

As with Britain in Bloom, we are advised by Clive Addison, one of the judges for the competition, who has been appointed Mentor to St. Brelade for their entry (and so will not take part in the assessment of St. Brelade) that "Environment not Bloom" and "Community" and "Quality of Life" for both residents and visitors head the criteria. The involvement of residents, the local authorities, and local companies, organizations and schools is of high importance.

The Mentoring process, to be provided by Clive Addison, is of much importance, as he will be there to follow the progress of planning, our emphasis on the best environmental, floral, educational, recycling, and sustainability projects and routes for the judges, presentations, publicity, publications and the appropriate entertainment anticipated by the judges. He recommends three mentoring visits which will be part of the total cost noted above. Any accommodation offered by residents will help control costs.

Entry forms are due now, but specifically the decision to enter needs to be resolved by the beginning of the year. The

Identity Form, describing the community, is needed by the beginning of February in time for the Judges to meet on 6th – 8th February. Judging takes place in late July, 2010.

Before the Judges reach Jersey, they need to receive Tourist/General Information about St. Brelade and Jersey as a whole. And how St. Brelade fits into the overall island picture. This can be existing publications of Island Tourism and of St. Brelade, extracted from St. Brelade or Britain in Bloom. It is needed for the meeting on 6th February.

A preliminary Portfolio is then prepared and published to reach the organizers by the end of May. This can include a CD or DVD, but it would be an introductory portfolio with the strategy of the Village, with reference to sustainability, energy saving, and biodiversity, not just horticulture.

Because of the European dimension of the competition, in every usage, Metric Measure, Euros, and use of the words Local People, not Community (which means Local Authority in some European languages) should be used. English is the language of the Judges, but our Mentor suggest that some translation into Italian would be popular, but not essential.

The Presentation, Brochure and the Judges' tour: These require meticulous planning and preparation and nothing less than a full dress rehearsal of the vehicle and facilities on the tour, the timing step by step, unloading and reloading times, a lunch break of one full hour, convenience stops, coffee breaks, at points where this can combine with assessment of a site and, above all, time to catch up when time is lost somewhere en route. Starting and finishing on time is essential. Judges have to visit every Town and Village entering the competition.

Criteria

This is clearly set out in the Judges point system and that needs to be the basis of emphasis in presentations and the tour. Too much time on a low scoring site or activity is unwise.

There are some curious points in the guidelines; A visit to a church, a cemetery, an Eco School, to a heritage site, to a site of architectural interest, a point about town planning, dealing with potential global warming related floods or improvements to road safety and recent benefits for tourists, evidence of local company involvement in volunteering, and how do we treat litter mongers.

Publicity

The more publicity before, and during the competition we can generate the more the Judges will see respect for their work and for the competition. Extolling the difference of Jersey from other countries which enter is well regarded: Lots of flags and Entente Florale banners. Radio interviews, Jersey Television to bring out the populace to be there while the judges are in town. Shops showing interest with window dressing, roadside advertisements, and welcoming notices in shops. All can help, but none are essential if the judges really find something special under the criteria in St. Brelade. Attendance of The Connetable to greet the Judges, or take part in a welcoming entertainment, so also attendance at some point of The Governor, or Bailiff. Judges like to find a real welcome, but that is not what they are judging.

Flowers—Sweet smell of Success: Kenya's Flower Exports

Exports of cut flowers from Kenya have again reached record levels with 2004 results posting a 44.7% increase over the previous year in volume terms. Actual export value rose by some 13.5% over the same period, making Kenya's horticulture sector the country's second largest foreign exchange earner, after tea, with more than $250m.

Announcing these results in London at the annual Kenya Flower Day, Erastus Mureithi, chairman of the Kenya Flower Council reported that Kenya exported over 88 tons of flowers last year, representing more than a doubling of exports in the past three years since 2001.

The Kenya Flower Council is a voluntary association that currently has a membership of 45 independent grower and export companies that accounts for around 70% of Kenya's exports of cut flowers.

Speaking at the Kenya Flower Day, Kenya's High Commissioner to the UK, Joseph Muchemi, pointed out that British Prime Minister Tony Blair's Commission for Africa report initiative "had stressed the need for success stories from Africa be highlighted as part of better balanced reporting of Africa, and one of the success stories mentioned in the report is the Kenya flower industry".

Echoing the High Commissioner's words, Mureithi said that Kenya's flower industry is an African success story and an example of how trade rather than aid can generate business and jobs in a country that encourages private sector initiative.

Challenges and Opportunities for Organic Sector in Ireland

The area under organic production in Ireland has doubled during the past decade. There are now 1,632 organic producers in Ireland farming a total area of 52,390 hectares, representing approximately 1.2 per cent of the total agricultural area. Teagasc organic adviser Pat Barry outlined the current position in his address to the Teagasc Organic Conference in Birr, County Offaly, today.

Teagasc Director Professor Gerry Boyle said: "The Recent Food Harvest 2020 committee endorsed the targets set out in Programme for Government. An increase in organic land use to five per cent from the current level of just over one per cent, which is ambitious and will require actions in a number of areas including promotion, marketing, innovation, research and product development."

The conference, which is focusing on the challenges and opportunities for organic producers, was officially opened by the Minister for Sustainable Transport, Horticulture and Planning, Ciaran Cuffe TD. Addressing the delegates he said;

"I am confident that the domestic and export opportunities that exist will provide reward for all the hard work, time and effort. My primary objective is to encourage farmers to take advantage of domestic and export opportunities for organic produce and, by doing so to maximise their potential income."

Over 1,500 farmers have attended farm walks organised by Teagasc this year, demonstrating organic farming in practise. Professor Boyle told the conference that Teagasc intend to use the BETTER Farm Programme to transfer knowledge to organic producers in the near future. He also pointed out that over 400 farmers have completed 25-hour FETAC accredited courses in the past 12 months and Teagasc will be offering these courses again nationwide over the coming months.

At the conference Teagasc launched a new DVD, "The Organic Option – Success Stories", which features case studies of organic farmers across the country. It showcases organic farming in practise and the farmers' testimonials will be very useful in the future to encourage others into organic farming.

The market opportunities for Irish organic beef were outlined by John Purcell, of Good Herdsmen. He pointed out that organic meat processors don't need to look any further than mainland Europe to find secure markets. Currently the Irish market consumes the meat from 2,500 organic cattle per year. But there is the potential to export 10,000 cattle to export markets. To meet this demand there is an opportunity for suckling and beef farmers to supply an extra 6,000 cattle to make a strong presence on the European market.

Current statistics would indicate that there are nearly 27,000 organic lambs produced in Ireland. But more than half the organic lamb is produced during July, August, and September. Lack of supply is identified as a major problem during the first half of the year.

The Irish organic food market is estimated to be worth €90 million with fruit and vegetables accounting for 35 per cent of total organic sales and yoghurt sales account for over 17 per cent.

CHAPTER–14

INSURANCE & LIABILITY ISSUES FOR OPERATORS

Whether it is hiring staff for a rural wedding, hiring helpers to staff your Halloween haunted forest or bringing in guides and bird dogs for your hunting preserve clients, you should be aware of the differences between employees and independent contractors. For farm or ranch bed and breakfast businesses, hunting preserves and nature tourism operations, this is an important question. Temporary employee status has important implications that raise several rather thorny issues. These include: taxes, workers compensation and workers-compensation insurance claims, general liability implications and general-liability insurance issues.

Let's look at the basic issue. Who is an employee? A good way to define this and get a handle on what level of decision-making is implied by their employment status. Essentially, anyone who performs a service to you under your direction or supervision is viewed as an employee; this means that you control what they do and how they should execute the task. This will be carried over to the setting of their work hours, training and you as employer having immediate power to hire and fire them.

Good employees are an almost priceless asset, but bad employees are a drain on your time and monetary resources and a potential source of an almost unlimited number of problems. There is one undeniable disadvantage of having employees, good or bad, and this is that there are unavoidable expenses related to them. If you have employees, you must pay various taxes, and in some cases, provide clothing and equipment and perhaps medical and dental coverage. At the very least, this means that you must withhold and pay Social Security and Medicare taxes, withhold federal and perhaps state income taxes, and pay unemployment tax on all wages paid to the employee.

Some employers try to get around the expense of having employees by hiring key services and not-so-critical staff as independent contractors. This can be an efficient, cost-effective business strategy, but confusing an employee with a contractor can be a mistake that can create serious insurance coverage, liability and other problems. It pays to take some time to carefully consider the role played by these individuals, their overall contributions and importance to your business, and what and where real value is within your business to you and your customers. Consider how potential cost-saving strategies impact long-term business performance. It may not be in your best interest to unnecessarily pay taxes and expend money or other expenses on a person if they are comfortable with providing a service as an independent contractor. However, if you incorrectly classify an employee as an independent contractor, that mistake may make you liable for employment taxes and additional penalties later on down the road or potentially expose you to otherwise avoidable legal action.

So, it is best to figure out who can be classified as an independent contractor and who is clearly an employee. A really good test is to ask yourself to what extent you, the employer, have the means, methods and the right and ability to control or direct the outcome of the work undertaken by the individual. This is what the Internal Revenue Service, judges, lawyers or juries will look at to test the degree to which owner/management controls the individual. The key here is "control of worker process and schedule."

For example, let's consider a rather simple situation where an individual on a ranch is tasked with taking hunters on horseback into the backcountry, guiding the hunt, taking care of their needs while in the bush and returning them safely to the ranch office on a specific date. This individual obviously is operating as an independent contractor. The contractor is in complete control of how tasks will be accomplished and the event timeline while in the field with the ranch's clients. In contrast, a person coming onto the ranch to provide housekeeping and cooking services in the ranch-house guest facilities for paying guests who are hunting on the ranch would be classified as an employee. This individual is responding to the schedule, decision making and immediate needs and oversight of the owner/manager.

Keeping with our on-ranch hunting party example, it is not unusual for licensed and bonded professional outfitters to have their own logistics staff, as well as to subcontract housekeeping, camp support, wrangling and other services to part-time employees or other independent contractors. In their contractual arrangement with the owner/managers of the ranch, the primary outfitter may provide any number of services to the guests, including providing off-site lodging, transportation in the field or to air connections, wranglers for horse-back transportation and camp services, game care and trophy preparation and other duties.

The ranch ownership and personnel do not have to be involved with any of this. In this case, working with a qualified professional independent contractor is a convenient and cost-effective arrangement for the ranch, the contractor and their employees and subcontractors and the ranch's guests. First and foremost, the outdoor business venture, like many other business models, hinges on the perception of quality and attention to detail experienced by the client (guest). Hiring a professional with which to consult and for delivery of key services may well be the best business strategy and most elegantly simplistic business choice for the ranch. The ranch need only respond to the preplanned and perhaps contractual needs of the contractor to ensure that the guest has a quality experience. Obviously, the independent contractor is performing more than one important function and is responsible for a great deal of planning and independent decision making. Also, the contractor is the most immediate, directly responsible party who sees to the needs and ensures the health and safety of the client.

However, it is important to remember that working with an independent contractor does not absolve a landowner of liability. In what the law calls "vicarious liability," a landowner is responsible for his or her own actions and also for those of people acting on the landowner's behalf. In other words, you are responsible for the actions of your employees and of independent contractors, like the pack guides in our example. This exposure risk usually is addressed through the contract with the guide service, a liability waiver signed by the visitor and the proper insurance coverage.

A written contract that details the arrangement and clearly addresses liability and tax issues should be in place and reviewed by the owner-manager's and the independent contractor's certified public accountants and perhaps their attorneys. The key element of any waiver is the "indemnity by user" clause. This usually is a very specific statement "that the user agrees to indemnify and hold harmless the landowner from any claims made by the user or third parties arising from the use of the land or activities."

Although contracts and waivers do not absolve you of responsibility for your guest's health and safety, they are legal documents valid in a court of law. With respect to liability waivers, each state treats them with different legal weight; have yours reviewed by your attorney or insurance provider as a part of your business' "risk-management assessment" and be sure to include them in your business planning and written business plan.

Liability waivers are common to most "high-risk" outdoor activities (horse-back riding, hunting, canoeing, kayaking, scuba and skin-diving, climbing, sky diving and parasailing) and have an important, often overlooked value of being a "reality check" for your guest. Seeing some of the risks of their activity spelled out before them and defining some of their responsibility for the soundness of their actions should make them a bit more thoughtful and safety conscious. An example of a waiver is provided for your review below; others can be found elsewhere on AgMRC in some of the references noted at the end of this article.

Converse to our hunting-guide independent-contractor example, there are many other types of businesses where guests (clients) are visiting farms and ranches. In most of these businesses, they will be served by an employee acting under the specific instructions, scheduling and oversight provided of the owner-manager or a senior employee. Employer-employee relationships may also be delineated by a written contract for the service or services provided. This is of course a very different relationship than the independent contractor and owner-manager one, and the two should not be confused. Simply because there is a contractual agreement, does not automatically qualify the employee as an independent contractor.

So what are the liability implications? With respect to general liability and liability insurance, it is highly unlikely that your farm or ranch general liability insurance policy probably will not defend against or pay claims on behalf of your independent contractors. This means that if you are classifying your guide, horse wranglers or event staff as independent contractors, and they are deemed to be the cause of an accident and litigation ensues, your policy will not defend them. If they are found liable, they may be left to cover the legal cost of a defense, as well as any damages. The damages would, at the least, be life changing and catastrophic for their business. You too as the farm or ranch-owner may have some exposure. While it is unlikely, you could still end up in civil court and be forced to bear those costs.

It is wise and prudent to have clearly delineated contracts in place with your employees and independent contractors. Have these reviewed by outside reviewers. Your lawyer, certified public accountant and a representative from your insurance provider (probably not the same one who provides your general farm or ranch coverage, but one familiar with your type of agritourism enterprise) would be good to consider.

To minimize your exposure, you should always have a written contract with an indemnity provision in place with your independent contractor. An indemnity provision is roughly defined as a contractual agreement made between different parties to compensate for any damage or loss. It may include any or all of:

- Protection against future loss;
- Legal exemption from liability for damages (e.g., protection, as by insurance, from liabilities or penalties incurred by someone's actions;
- A sum of money paid in compensation for loss or injury (aka "damages");
- Something paid by way of such compensation; and
- With respect to our greater society, the legal exemption from penalties attaching to unconstitutional or illegal actions, granted to public officers and other persons. For example, as commonly employed in the wording of most insurance policies, "the company will indemnify the policy holder for any losses for which they are insured."

Also, require the independent contractor to maintain their own liability insurance if they are able to do so and have them submit written proof of this to you, as well as their statement that they are responsible for their worker's compensation insurance. Understandably, this is not always possible; in these situations, you need to have your liability policy endorsed to cover your hunting guides as additional "insureds."

When you do this, it is best to consider a specialty insurance provider who understands outdoor and special-event coverage. This is far from some simple umbrella on an existing farm or ranch policy. Find a provider who understands your "exposures" (risks) and is not new to your type of venture. For example, one well-respected national company (hardly a recognized household-insurance "name" in the business) provides a range of services to the sport-hunting and outdoor-adventure community, clearly states that they understand the risks and coverage needs associated with unique exposures, "like hunting dogs in your care, custody and control; live birds held as stock; outfitters and guides; use of elevated hunting platforms; use of ATVs, tractors and off-road vehicles; trap and skeet ranges; and hunting lease agreements."

These specialty insurance firms are usually very helpful in providing and will provide various risk self-assessment tools, sample independent contractor agreements and liability waivers free-of-charge, as part of their support and customer service packages. They also can prove those "special endorsements" so important for coverage for or contracts with independent contractors. For example, if injured while working on your behalf, an independent contractor can bring suit against you, unlike employees that must use workers compensation insurance to remedy their loss. This increases your potential overall liability exposure. Your specialty-coverage insurance firm will be aware of this and have an endorsement in their policy to cover this exposure, can suggest wording for a waver-of-liability provision for your contract with the independent contractor and may have other strategies to mitigate this and other risks.

Many resources are available to agritourism, special-activity and special-event operators. These include national and state tourism and similar trade associations. Sample forms and discussions of employment, insurance and liability issues are available elsewhere on the Internet. They also are available in the pages of many agritourism, small-business-management and risk-management publications, including workbooks, planning guides and document templates available from the Extension services of most major land-grant universities, state and federal agencies and business-support organizations.

How you classify your workers, delineate their employment status (contracts) and their relationship with your guests (waivers); and consider the issues of taxes, workers compensation and workers-compensation insurance claims, general liability implications and general-liability insurance issues may seem like a real headache today but can result in a lot of peace of mind a little later down the road.

Additional Resources

- Agritourism and Nature Tourism in California, Ellie Rilla and Holly George, Agriculture and Natural Resources, University of California, 2005 - Chapter 5 considers liability, insurance and other risk-management issues. University of California Agriculture and Natural Resources Publication 3484. Agricultural and Natural Resources Publications, 1850 Research Park Drive, University of California, Davis, CA, 95616; 800-994-8849.
- Agritourism Workbook: Guide to Discovering New Ways to Build a Successful Agricultural Business Through Direct Farm Marketing, Britany Russel,

Agri-Business Council of Oregon, 2003 - Contains a nice summary of liability and insurance considerations that includes short and succinct discussions regarding invitees, licensees, trespassers, equine activity, alcoholic beverage consumption and many other topics. Publication from the Agri-Business Council of Oregon, 1200 NW Naito Parkway, Suite #290, Portland, OR 97209; 503-241-1487.

- Black's Win & Clay/Waterfowl - The "bible" of upland-bird-hunting preserve and lay-target shooting range operators and customers. This annual guidebook contains specialty insurance providers and concise discussions of liability and employee-classification issues. Grand View Media Group, 200 Croft Street, Suite 1, Birmingham, AL, 35242. Customer service can be reached at 800-766-0039 or via the E-mail link listed above.
- Gillingham & Associates, Westminster, Colorado - A division of Philadelphia Insurance Companies. Example of a well-established industry leader that is a provider for all sorts of hunting-outdoor related insurance needs related to guides and outfitters, landowners, guest ranches, bed & breakfast operations, lodges, hunt clubs and hunting leases, and special event coverage. Gillingham & Associates, 8501 Turnpike Drive, Suite 200, Westminster, CO 80031; 800-849-9288.
- Insuring "Agritainment": Is it Farming or a Business?, American Association of Insurance Services, 2005.
- The Legal Guide for Direct Farm Marketing, Drake University, Des Moines, Iowa - For more information, call: 515-271-2947.
- North American Farmers' Direct Marketing Association - This site provides a member's liability

insurance list. For more information, call: 413-529-0386.

- OutdoorInsurance.Com, Wheeling, West Virginia - Example of a provider for all sorts of hunting-outdoor related insurance needs. Site contains many sample forms and discussion related to guides and outfitters, landowners, special event coverage and property and equipment forms. R. Tim Reed, P.O. Box 6336, Wheeling, WV 26003; 866-695-9040; tim@outdoorsinsurance.com.
- Outdoor Insurance Group, Wichita, Kansas - Example of a provider for all sorts of hunting-outdoor related insurance needs. Site contains many sample forms and discussion related to guides and outfitters, landowners, guest ranches, bed & breakfast operations, recreational-vehicle parks and campgrounds, off-road vehicle use and rental, hunt clubs and hunting leases, special event coverage and property and equipment forms. Outdoor Insurance Group, 400 N. Woodlawn Suite 100, Wichita, KS 67208; 888-683-7808.
- Understanding Farmers Comprehensive Personal Liability Policy: A Guide for Farmers, Attorneys and Insurance Agents, National Center for Agricultural Law, Research & Information, School of Law, University of Arkansas - For more information, call: 479-575-7646.

INSURANCE OPTIONS FOR NATURE BASED OPERATORS

As Nature Based tourism operators, it is important not only to secure our land base, but also to ensure a sustainable future of our industry by protecting against foreseen and unforeseen risk. The Wilderness Tourism Association recognizes the need for accessible coverage at a reasonable cost to the operators, no matter the size of their organization.

The WTA uses Jardine Lloyd Thompson for its own liability coverage (as do many organizations in our sector) and has found them to offer good coverage and competitive rates, and to have great customer service. Contact Angela Dunlop MacKenzie and indicate that you are a member of WTA.

Gardener Insurance

Even if everything in the garden is coming up roses and you have a full order book of work from already contented customers - in fact, *particularly* if you have a full order book of work from already contented customers - you need gardeners insurance.

Because the busier you are, the more tempted you'll be to cut the odd corner. And that's when accidents happen. You're not as careful as you might be whilst digging a trench and you rupture a mains water pipe. You'll be responsible for all the associated repair costs.

You're not as conscientious as you might be about fixing a loose slab in a path and a customer breaks her ankle tripping over it. You could find yourself on the wrong end of a substantial claim for compensation. You're not as alert as you should be to a trainee assistant who cuts himself badly whilst cleaning a lawnmower. You could be sued.

It only takes a single incident like any of the above and, suddenly, everything you've been working for could be put at risk. Forget the plans for expansion, the new kitchen, the dream holiday. You'll be struggling to find the money to meet the terms of a court order and pay the lawyers' bills. Unless, of course, you have proper gardener insurance which includes public liability and employers' liability. Because then you'll be covered for all those unexpected costs that could, quite literally, put you out of business.

The best news is that the peace of mind that gardeners insurance offers doesn't have to be expensive. As you'll discover if you follow the link to find the insurance for gardeners that's right for you and your business.

OAMPS Tourism Industry Insurance

OAMPS Tourism Industry Insurance provides a broad and flexible range of insurance cover for tourism operators and the recreation industry.

OAMPS Insurance Brokers offer a competitively priced and comprehensive insurance solution for tourism and recreation businesses. Our tourism industry insurance products have the backing from many of the major tourism industry bodies including Tourism Alliance Victoria, Tourism Industry Council Tasmania and the Queensland Tourism Industry Council.

Our specialist tourism industry insurance is designed for a broad range of activities, including:

1. Public and product liability Commercial motor (e.g. 4WD's, buses, etc.) Charter boats Office and general business insurance
2. Sightseeing tours of all kinds Snowskiing and snow activities 4WD and bushwalking tours Camping tours and accommodation Canoeing and kayaking activities

1. Corporate travel Group personal accident Workers' compensation Risk management
2. Mobile animal farms Surf schools and safaris Kiteboarding instruction and tours Eco tours and nature-based tours Adventure tourism activities

New Insurance Cover for Kenya Tourism Operators

Hotels, lodges, safari camps and safari/tour operators can now up their insurance covers to internationally-acceptable levels, as a new cover is available through Kenyan insurers backed up through re-insurance arrangements with Lloyds in London. The risk mitigation policy was launched last week in Kenya as the second country in Africa after South Africa and will be adding another component to successfully promoting tourism to Kenya as added insurance security can now be offered to visitors.

In case of an accident in Kenya, safari/tour companies are often targeted with legal cases, as are hotels, resorts, and safari lodges/camps, and not always is such action brought in a Kenyan court but rather abroad, in the home country of the affected victim, a situation the new policy also addresses.

When making further inquiries, this correspondent was told that a range of activities will now be covered like game drives, game walks, the use of boats on rivers, or for fishing, including white water rafting, water sports activities as offered by coastal resorts, horse riding, and the risks in restaurants and hotels over food poisoning.

The new insurance policies are reportedly also covering legal fees; claims for wrongful death, injuries, and illness; and will complement existing insurances for the airlift and medical treatment of tourists, should this be required.

The leading stakeholders this correspondent subsequently was in touch with generally welcomed the new insurance options, although a few had issues over the cost, which in this correspondent's opinion would give Kenya a competitive edge over their regional competitors. In other countries across Eastern Africa, insurance covers are often laughably low, and in particular in regard of the liability of hotelkeepers, restricted to "peanuts" in line with age-old legislation and regulations. This then often leads to such cases being brought in overseas courts, where settlements and awards are predictably massive and could, in a worst case scenario, bankrupt a lodge, resort, hotel, or safari operators.

It could not be ascertained if the cover would or could be extended to other countries within the East African Community should operators ask for it through their own insurance companies.

AGREEMENT EXAMPLES

The following is an example of an Indemnification Agreement between a Midwestern bird-hunting hunt club and its clients. Each client is given a safety briefing and then asked to respond to the following document. It is provided here as a sample for your review and as an educational tool. (Use at your own risk):

Indemnification Agreement

Release of Liability:

I the undersigned, agree to hold <name of business> Hunt Club and it's owners, management, employees, agents and guides completely harmless and waive all claims of liability for any injury, accident or death resulting from any cause, whether natural or man-made.

In the event that I cause, or am alleged to have caused any injury, accident or death to another person or damages to another person's property, then I agree to indemnify and hold harmless from any claim against <name of business> Hunt Club and it's owners, management, employees, agents and guides.

I have read and fully understand the above release/ waiver and fully understand that I have given up substantial rights by voluntarily signing this document.

Signature________________________________

Date:________________

Signature of Parent or Guardian if under 18 years of age____________________

Name (first, middle, last) ______________________

Address (street, city, state, zip code) ______________

Home telephone number________________

Mobile phone number______________________________

E-mail address ____________________________

CHAPTER–15

HORTICULTURAL TOURISM : ZONING AND HEALTH

Zoning is "the division of a city or county by legislative regulations into areas (zones), specifying the uses allowable for the property in these areas". Zoning ordinances can often be seen as a hurdle for beginning agritourism businesses. One survey found 13% of agritourism businesses surveyed had difficulties with zoning (University of Tennessee Extension 2005), and an online survey found that more than 50% had difficulties (Eckert 2007). Ordinances may prohibit particular commercial activities or require that specific facilities and/or structures be present. In some regions, ordinances have been altered to be more accommodating for farms involved in agritourism.

Zoning ordinances are generally handled by county or municipal governments. You can contact these entities to determine which ordinances may be in place in your area. The nature of zoning ordinances and the ability to obtain zoning variances will vary greatly with each locality. For a discussion of zoning and home-based businesses visit

Examples of Zoning Ordinances: Limiting or prohibiting specific commercial recreational activities in an area. Requiring flush toilets and other facilities for sanitation

Prohibiting attractions, restaurants, or bed and breakfasts in certain areas Regulating location and size of structures.

HEALTH CONSIDERATIONS

Like zoning, there are legislative regulations in place aimed at protecting the health of both individuals and the environment. Health regulations will vary from place to place, but generally your county/local health department will handle these. Food preparation and safety, and waste disposal regulations, are often especially important considerations. Licenses and permits are generally required. Your County/Local Extension Agent should be able to provide the necessary information.

Examples of Health Regulations: Limiting the number of visitors allowed on a "home stay" farm or ranch Requiring one or more persons involved with food preparation or handling to obtain food handlers' permits or certificates Requiring certain types of equipment needed for food storage Requiring a certain amount of drinking water be available for visitors and placing requirements on water quality

Zoning Schemes

Zoning schemes provide a spatial differentiation of protected areas based on different objectives of management. In Western Australia, four different zones are widely applied in national parks: special conservation, wilderness, natural environment and recreation. Special conservation zones have high nature conservation values and may be closed to public use.

East Wanneroo Land Use and Water Management Strategy

Three draft land use scenarios are presented to provide preliminary ideas and promote community discussion on possible options. East Wanneroo Land Use and Water Management Strategy Community Forum 29 November 2004 Progress Report.

This preliminary discussion paper is being released by the community consultative committee to allow the community to provide input into the planning process prior to the WAPC formally considering these proposals.

The planning scenarios contained in this preliminary discussion paper have not been considered or endorsed by the WAPC, the City of Wanneroo, the Department of Environment or the Department of Agriculture.

Community Forum 29 November 2004 Progress Report

The East Wanneroo Land Use and Water Management Strategy (EWLUWMS) is being prepared to address the issues raised through the consideration of subdivision appeals by the Minister for Planning and Infrastructure and by the local member Mrs Dianne Guise MLA, the City of Wanneroo and the east Wanneroo local community about the impact that current water availability, allocation, and land use planning is having on the owners of rural properties and development options in the east Wanneroo area.

The key issues to be resolved by the strategy are:

- Which future land use options will achieve the desired environmental, economic and social outcomes for the benefit of the whole community.
- The identification of some form of future land development opportunities.
- The mechanisms needed to allow the continuation and expansion of the existing agricultural industry and local economy that is currently based on the use of the limited groundwater from the Gnangara Mound.
- How to apply a whole of government approach to land use planning, groundwater management and pine plantation clearing to manage land use change and groundwater demands for public drinking water, private agricultural uses and environmental water requirements.

The Community Consultative Committee, established to assist the EWLUWMS preparation, released a preliminary discussion paper entitled 'East Wanneroo Land Use and Water Management Strategy' in May 2004 to allow the community to provide input into the planning process prior to the Western Australian Planning Commission (WAPC) formally considering these proposals.

Three draft land use scenarios were presented to provide preliminary ideas and promote community discussion on possible options for the future development, land use and water management measures that may be appropriate for the east Wanneroo area.

Some 432 submissions were received expressing a wide range of views including:

- Retaining the rural lifestyle and amenity - no future urban zoning.
- Retaining the rural lifestyle but wanting some form of future rural subdivision.
- Support for future urban zoning as in either scenarios 1, 2 or 3, or combinations of the three.
- Suggested additional urban areas in the Gnangara area.
- Protecting the environment and lakes.

In summary the submissions were:

Support of some land use change = 258 Opposed to land use change = 174

The following is an approximate breakdown but some submissions were not entirely clear about what scenario was favoured.

Scenario 1	Scenario 2	Scenario 3	Scenario 1/2	Scenario 2/3
82	22	32	16	98

No Support for Scenarios 1,2,or 3 - 159

Did not say or unclear - 23

The conclusions drawn from the submissions are:

- It is clear that a change in land use was supported; a question is how much, where and when.
- A large number of land owners around Lake Mariginiup were opposed to future urban zoning and an increase in the parks and recreation reservations around Lake Mariginiup.
- Large numbers of landowners in the Gnangara area wanted future urban zoning.

Note: These were counted as no support to either scenario 1, 2 or 3.

Wanneroo Community Forum - 29 November 2004

A community forum, chaired by Mrs Dianne Guise MLA, was held at the City of Wanneroo on Monday 29 November to progress community input to the strategy. A new land use scenario plan was presented.

The plan showed:

- Possible future urban areas in south-east Wanneroo.
- Possible rural living subdivision areas. • Protection of the wetlands.
- Retaining rural land in the north in Carabooda and Nowergup, recognising the basic raw material areas in Nowergup, and the landscape values of the strip of undulating limestone and tuarts along the Gibbs Road area.
- Introducing the concept of creating new agricultural and horticultural areas north-east of Carabooda in the state forest after the pines are removed. This would replace the horticultural land lost to the south as a result of any possible future urban development and supplement the existing areas at Carabooda.

The new agricultural and horticultural areas would be supplied with a water supply based on using recycled treated waste water from the Beenyup and future Alkimos Waste Water Treatment Plants. This is a medium to long-term proposal that needs to be investigated in more detail and is feasible as urban development and population growth occurs in the north-west urban corridor, which in turn provides more opportunities to use recycled waste water. Nevertheless, there are still many economic, social, health and environmental issues to consider and resolve.

This plan will now be subject to further investigation by government agencies and the City of Wanneroo. It is a working draft and will be subject to change.

Proposed Land Use Scenario Plan

The 115 participants at the community forum were presented with information from the Department of Environment, the Department of Agriculture, the Department for Planning and Infrastructure and from a vegetable growers perspective. Participants were asked to consider the new plan and list important key issues under the heading of five topics.

Topic 1 - Groundwater Management and Environment

Topic 2 - Horticulture and Agriculture Land Use

Topic 3 - Possible future Urban Land Uses

Topic 4 - Rural Living Subdivision

Topic 5 - Tourism and Heritage Values

EWLUWM Strategy Direction

An integrated strategy for the east Wanneroo area and the Gnangara Mound needs to be formulated to accommodate all the competing demands on the Gnangara Mound groundwater resource.

A new land use concept for the east Wanneroo area is proposed. The concept is based on creating new urban areas in south-east Wanneroo, retaining rural land in the north and establishing new agricultural areas to the east of Carabooda to replace the areas lost to urbanisation. This concept is based on using fit for purpose recycled water from the Beenyup and future Alkimos treatment plants to supply recycled water (independent of rainfall) for agricultural and horticultural purposes.

The additional new agricultural areas will need to be leasehold in tenure, with a recycled water allocation tied to the lease. In this way, there is a guarantee that the land will always be used for horticultural purposes, and in this way justifies the capital cost of installing a recycled waste water scheme.

The use of recycled water can also supplement the environmental water requirements for the Yanchep cave system and Wanneroo wetlands and, in concert with the controlled clearing and thinning of the pine plantations, buffer the impact of the predicted lower rainfall conditions and falling groundwater levels.

A recycled water scheme and the staged removal of the pine plantations would also reduce the competition for limited groundwater resources between the Water Corporation and private users, thereby augmenting the public drinking water scheme.

However, there are still many planning, health and technical issues to be more fully investigated and resolved.

To achieve this, a whole of government and coordinated approach to the management of the land and water resources of the Gnangara Mound is needed to deliver a sustainable solution to all the competing demands on the groundwater resource to all sectors of the community.

This is a significant opportunity to put into action some of the principles of sustainable environmental management of land, water and agricultural resources that are promoted in the State Sustainability Strategy, the State Water Strategy and the State Planning Strategy.

Where to From here?

A final draft Strategy will be prepared for endorsement by the WAPC and the City of Wanneroo. (1st Qtr 2005)

Consideration of the final draft Strategy will include release for a formal public consultation period.

The final Strategy will then be released by the Government, WAPC and City of Wanneroo.

If you require further information please contact the Western Australian Planning Commission on 9264 7777.

BIBLIOGRAPHY

- Aitken, Richard & Looker, Michael (2002). *The Oxford Companion to Australian Gardens*. Melbourne: Oxford University Press. ISBN 0195536444.

- Alter, Judy (1997). *Amusement Parks*. New York: Franklin Watts. ISBN 0531203042.

- Bailey, Liberty Hyde & Bailey, Ethel Z. (1978). *Hortus Third*. New York: Macmillan. ISBN 0025054708.

- Bean, A.R. (editor) (2006). *Collecting and preserving plant specimens, A Manual*. Queensland Herbarium, Environmental Protection Agency Biodiversity Sciences unit, Brisbane.. ISBN 1-920928-06-5.

- Bright, Randy (1987). *Disneyland: Inside Story*. Harry N. Abrams. ISBN 978-0810908116.

- Davis, James D. (2007). "Holyland theme park". *Sun Sentinel* (Tribune Company). http://www.southflorida.com/travel/sfl-holyland,0,7964224.story.

- Desmond, Ray (2007). *The History of the Royal Botanic Gardens Kew*. London: Kew Publishing. ISBN 9781842461686.

- Drayton, Richard (2000). *Nature's Government: Science, Imperial Britain, and the 'Improvement' of the World*. London: Yale University Press. ISBN 0300059760.

- Frances, Chamberlain (November 4, 2001). "The View From/Waterbury; A Hilltop Landmark Undergoes a Revival". *The New York Times*.

- Guerra, Francisco (1966). "Aztec Medicine". *Medical History* **10** (4): 315 – 338. http://www.ncbi.nlm.nih.gov:80/pmc/articles/PMC1033639/pdf/medhist00149-0009.pdf. Retrieved 2009-11-21.

- Heutte, Fred (1872). "A New Concept: the Commercial Botanical Garden". *American Horticulturalist* **51** (2): 14 – 17.

- Heywood, Vernon H. (1987). "The changing rôle of the botanic gardens". In Bramwell, David et. al. (eds). *Botanic Gardens and the World Conservation Strategy*. London: Academic Press. pp. 3 – 18. ISBN 0121254623.

- Hill, Arthur W. (1915). "The History and Functions of Botanic Gardens". *Annals of the Missouri Botanical Garden* **2** (1/2): 185 – 240. doi:10.2307/2990033. http://jstor.org/stable/2990033.

- Holmes, Edward M. (1906). "Horticulture in Relation to Medicine". *Journal of the Royal Horticultural Society* **31**: 42 – 61.

- Huxley, Anthony (ed. in chief) (1992). *The New Royal Horticultural Society Dictionary of Gardening*. London: Macmillan. ISBN 1561590010.

- Hyams, Edward & MacQuitty, William (1969). *Great Botanical Gardens of the World*. London: Bloomsbury Books. ISBN 0906223733.

- July 2008, Disney & Co., Six Flags, And Other U.S. Theme And Amusement Park Operators Look To Drive Up Revenue With Foreign Visitors, *IBISWorld*

- McGee, J.R. and Kruse, M. (1986) Swidden horticulture among the Lacandon Maya [videorecording (29 mins.)]. University of California, Berkeley: Extension Media Center

- Minter, Sue (2000). *The Apothecaries' Garden*. Stroud, UK: Sutton Publishing. ISBN 9780750924498.
- Mueller, Ferdinand von (1871). *The objects of a botanic garden in relation to industries : a lecture delivered at the Industrial and Technological Museum*. Melbourne: Mason, Firth & McCutcheon.
- Ogilvie, Brian W. (2006). *The Science of Describing: Natural History in Renaissance Europe*. Chicago: University of Chicago Press. ISBN 9780226620879.
- Rutherford, Scott (2000). *The American Roller Coaster*. Osceola, WI: MBI Publishing Company. ISBN 0760306893.
- Samuelson, Dale; Wendy Yegoiants (2001). *The American Amusement Park*. St. Paul, MN: MBI Publishing Company. ISBN 0760309817.
- Simmons, John B. et al. (eds) (1976). *Conservation of Threatened Plants*. London: Plenum Press. ISBN 0306328011.
- Taylor, Patrick (2006). *The Oxford Companion to the Garden*. Oxford: Oxford University Press. ISBN 9780198662556.
- Thanos, C.A. (2005). "The Geography of Theophrastus' Life and of his Botanical Writings (Ðåñé Öõôùí)". In Karamanos, A.J. & Thanos, C.A. (eds). *Biodiversity and Natural Heritage in the Aegean, Proceedings of the Conference 'Theophrastus 2000' (Eressos - Sigri, Lesbos, July 6 – 8, 2000)*. Athens: Fragoudis. pp. 23 – 45. http://www.biology.uoa.gr/~cthanos/Papers/Theophrastus%20Geography.pdf.
- Thompson, S.I. (1977) Women, Horticulture, and Society in Tropical America. American Anthropologist, N.S., 79: 908-910
- von Hagen, V.W. (1957) The Ancient Sun Kingdoms Of The Americas. Ohio: The World Publishing Company
- Wyse Jackson, Peter S. & Sutherland, Lucy A. (2000) *International Agenda for Botanic Gardens in Conservation*

Richmond, UK: Botanic Gardens Conservation International. http://www.bcn.es/medciencies/botanicgardens2004/abstracts/pdf_publicacions/IntenationaAgenda.pdf.

- Wyse Jackson, Peter S. (1999). "Experimentation on a Large Scale – An Analysis of the Holdings and Resources of Botanic Gardens". *BGCNews* (Richmond, UK: Botanic Gardens Conservation International) 3 (3): 53 – 72. http://www.bgci.org/resources/article/0080.

- Young, Michael (1987). *Collins Guide to the Botanical Gardens of Britain*. London: Collins. ISBN 0002182130.

INDEX

R

S

T

U

V

W

X

Z